Landeskunde aktiv
Discovering Great Britain

Jennifer Easterbrook, Jennifer Mock,
Andreas Redl

Landeskunde aktiv
Discovering Great Britain

Bildquellennachweis

Cover iStockphoto (dynasoar), Calgary, Alberta; **Cover** Shutterstock (Jo millington), New York; **Cover** Shutterstock (michaeljung), New York; **Cover** Shutterstock (duchy), New York; **Cover** Shutterstock (PHOTOCREO Michal Bednarek), New York; **KV** 5b Bild 1 Shutterstock (juefraphoto), New York; **KV** 5b Bild 2 Shutterstock (BLACKDAY), New York; **KV** 5b Bild 3 Shutterstock (Peter Zvonar), New York; **KV** 5b Bild 4 Shutterstock (Olga Nayashkova), New York; **KV9b** Bild 6 Shutterstock (browndogstudios), New York; **KV** 5b Bild 5 Shutterstock (hlphoto), New York; **KV** 5b Bild 6 Shutterstock (ElenaGaak), New York; **KV** 5b Bild 7 Shutterstock (Olga Nayashkova), New York; **KV** 9b Bild 1 Shutterstock (AkeSak), New York; **KV9b** Bild 2 Shutterstock (Miguel Angel Salinas Salinas), New York; **KV9b** Bild 3 Shutterstock (Tashal), New York; **KV9b** Bild 4 Shutterstock (ankudi), New York; **KV9b** Bild 5 Shutterstock (ulia_lavrova), New York; **KV** 12c Shutterstock (schab), New York; **KV** 2 Klett-Archiv , Stuttgart; **KV** 3 Bild 2 Fotolia.com (chas53), New York; **KV** 3 Bild 1 Dreamstime.com (Vatikaki), Brentwood, TN; **KV** 5 Bild 2 Shutterstock (Joe Gough), New York; **KV** 5 Bild 7 Klett-Archiv (Jennifer Easterbrook), Stuttgart; **KV** 5 Bild 6 Klett-Archiv (Jennifer Easterbrook), Stuttgart; **KV** 5 Bild 5 Klett-Archiv (Jennifer Easterbrook), Stuttgart; **KV** 5 Bild 4 Fotolia.com (stocksolutions), New York; **KV** 5 Bild 1 Shutterstock (Envyligh), New York; **KV** 5 Bild 3 Shutterstock (threeseven), New York; **KV** 6 iStockphoto (Danielrao), Calgary, Alberta; **KV** 7 Shutterstock (Joe Gough), New York; **KV** 10 Fotolia.com (Claudio Divizia), New York; **KV** 12 Illustration Matthias Pflügner , Berlin; **KV** 13 Bild 2 iStockphoto (DavidCallan), Calgary, Alberta; **KV** 13 Bild 1 Fotolia.com (JiSign), New York; **KV** 14 und KV 14b Klett-Archiv (Jenni Mock), Stuttgart; **KV** 15 Illustration Matthias Pflügner , Berlin; **KV** 15 Fotolia.com (stocksolutions), New York; **KV** 16 und KV 23 ullstein bild (Granger, NYC), Berlin; **KV** 17 2 + online KV iStockphoto (Ljupco), Calgary, Alberta; **KV** 17 + online KV iStockphoto (coloroftime), Calgary, Alberta; **KV** 19 Bild 4 Shutterstock (Jerry Syder), New York; **KV** 19 Bild 3 Shutterstock (ian johnston), New York; **KV** 19 Bild 2 Fotolia.com (Sander Meertins), New York; **KV** 19 Bild 1 Fotolia.com (powell83), New York; **KV** 19 Bild 5 Shutterstock (Rainer Lesniewski), New York; **KV** 20 Shutterstock (Tanarch), New York; **KV** 22 Bild 2 Shutterstock (r.nagy), New York; **KV** 22 Bild 3 Shutterstock (Daniel Gale), New York; **KV** 22 Bild 1 Shutterstock (chrisdorney), New York; **KV** 23 Sven Palmowski , Barcelona; **KV** 25 (1) Shutterstock (L Galbraith), New York; **KV** 26 Shutterstock (Arndale), New York; **KV** 27 Shutterstock (Firma V), New York; **KV** 28 Bild1 Shutterstock (Ivica Drusany), New York; **KV** 28 Bild2 Shutterstock (Skully), New York; **KV** 28 Bild3 Shutterstock (Lifebrary), New York; **KV** 29 Bild2 Shutterstock (Denis Makarenko), New York; **KV** 29 Bild 3 Shutterstock (Shelly Wall), New York; **KV** 29 Bild4 Shutterstock (David Adamson), New York; **KV** 29 Bild1 Shutterstock (Maxisport), New York; **KV30** und KV30b Shutterstock (H Cooper), New York; **KV** 31 Bild 3 Shutterstock (Matthew Dixon), New York; **KV** 31 Bild 2 Shutterstock (Philip Bird LRPS CPAGB), New York; **KV** 31 Bild 1 Alamy (James Davies), Abingdon, Oxfordshire; **KV** 33 Bild 2 Shutterstock (Bikeworldtravel), New York; **KV** 33 Bild 1 Shutterstock (Bikeworldtravel), New York; **KV** 33 Bild 3 Alamy (Alistair Laming), Abingdon, Oxfordshire; **KV** 34 Shutterstock (PRABHAS ROY), New York; **KV** 35 Bild 2 Shutterstock (Viktor Kovalenko), New York; **KV** 35 Bild 1 Shutterstock (Bikeworldtravel), New York

1. Auflage   1⁵ ⁴ ³ ² ¹ | 2020 19 18 17 16

Alle Drucke dieser Auflage sind unverändert und können im Unterricht nebeneinander verwendet werden.
Die letzte Zahl bezeichnet das Jahr des Druckes. Das Werk und seine Teile sind urheberrechtlich geschützt. Jede Nutzung in anderen als den gesetzlich zugelassenen Fällen bedarf der vorherigen schriftlichen Einwilligung des Verlags. Hinweis zu § 52 a UrhG: Weder das Werk noch seine Teile dürfen ohne eine solche Einwilligung eingescannt und in ein Netzwerk eingestellt werden. Dies gilt auch für Intranets von Schulen und sonstigen Bildungseinrichtungen. Fotomechanische oder andere Wiedergabeverfahren nur mit Genehmigung des Verlags.
Die in diesem Werk angegebenen Links wurden von der Redaktion sorgfältig geprüft, wohl wissend, dass sie sich ändern können. Die Redaktion erklärt hiermit ausdrücklich, dass zum Zeitpunkt der Linksetzung keine illegalen Inhalte auf den zu verlinkenden Seiten erkennbar waren. Auf die aktuelle und zukünftige Gestaltung, die Inhalte oder die Urheberschaft der verlinkten Seiten hat die Redaktion keinerlei Einfluss. Deshalb distanziert sie sich hiermit ausdrücklich von allen Inhalten aller verlinkten Seiten, die nach der Linksetzung verändert wurden. Diese Erklärung gilt für alle in diesem Werk aufgeführten Links.

© Ernst Klett Sprachen GmbH, Rotebühlstraße 77, 70178 Stuttgart, 2016.
Alle Rechte vorbehalten.
Internetadresse: www.klett-sprachen.de

Autoren: Jennifer Easterbrook, Jennifer Mock, Andreas Redl
Redaktion: Don Haupt
Layoutkonzeption: Maja Merz
Gestaltung und Satz: DOPPELPUNKT, Stuttgart
Umschlaggestaltung: Maja Merz
Druck und Bindung: CEWE Stiftung & Co. KGaA, Germering
Printed in Germany

ISBN 978-3-12-513582-6

Inhaltsverzeichnis

Kompetenz- / Themenraster 6

Vorwort 7

Abkürzungen und Symbole 7

Zusatzmaterialien online 7

Kopiervorlagen 8

Kommentar mit Lösungen 50

Kompetenz- / Themenraster

	Sprechen	Lesen	Schreiben	Hör-/Sehverstehen
Customs and traditions				
special events	1 British Christmas traditions 🗨	2 Guy Fawkes	3 Spooky Halloween	4 Merry Christmas!
food and drinks	5 British food	6 Tea Time	7 A British recipe – Shepherd's Pie 🗨	8 British food culture
History				
people	9 Growing up royal	10 William Shakespeare – world-famous writer	11 Conversation with a Viking	12 Sherlock Holmes – Mrs Hudson's lucky day
places	13 A guided tour of the Tower of London 🗨	14 Stonehenge of Scotland	15 Romans in Britain – Life on Hadrian's Wall	16 Shakespeare's Globe
School and beyond				
	17 School uniforms – a necessary evil?	18 Sean's day at school	19 A school trip to the Isle of Wight	20 Geography lesson: The British Isles
Whereabouts				
London	21 Shopping in London	22 London Sights	23 Shakespeare's London 🗨	24 Getting around and finding your way
Edinburgh	25 Edinburgh Castle – a guided tour 🗨	26 Edinburgh Castle	27 Scottish words	28 The Edinburgh Fringe Festival
Wales	29 Welsh stars	30 The Welsh flag	31 Cardiff – Europe's youngest capital 🗨	32 King Arthur and Rhitta Gawr
Multicultural Britain				
	33 A trip to Chinatown	34 A story of success	35 The Notting Hill Carnival 🗨	36 Multicultural influences in Britain
Games				
	37 London Jeopardy	38 A day in the life of a British girl	39 Guess the word	40 Snap it!

🗨 Mediation

Vorwort

Wer kennt sie nicht: die verzweifelte Suche nach landeskundlichem Unterrichtsmaterial, das schon für den Unterricht aufbereitet wurde und eine sinnvolle Ergänzung zum Lehrwerk bietet. Der vorliegende Band der Reihe *Landeskunde Aktiv* will Englischlehrer/innen genau an dieser Stelle entlasten.

Discovering Great Britain enthält im ersten Abschnitt sorgfältig durchdachte und im Unterricht erprobte Arbeitsblätter, die verschiedene landeskundliche Aspekte Großbritanniens für die Klassen 6 und 7 behandeln. Die Kopiervorlagen sind dabei *ready to teach*, das heißt, dass sie für den spontanen Gebrauch (also auch für eine Vertretungsstunde) geeignet sind.

Jedes Arbeitsblatt legt dabei den Fokus auf eine im Englischunterricht zentralen Kompetenzen *(Sprechen, Lesen, Schreiben, Hör-/Sehverstehen)*, so dass es nicht nur einen landeskundlichen Ansatz bietet, sondern gleichzeitig auch zur Schulung der jeweiligen Kompetenz verwendet werden kann. Aufgaben zur Sprachmittlung finden sich auf die einzelnen Kompetenzen verteilt wieder. Die Arbeitsblätter berücksichtigen außerdem die verschiedenen Sozialformen des Unterrichts. Auch spielerische Arbeitsaufträge – etwa für Abschlussstunden – haben ihren Eingang in diesen Band gefunden.

Darüber hinaus sind die Arbeitsblätter thematisch gruppiert. Sie können entweder einzeln als Ergänzung zum Lehrwerk eingesetzt oder aber auch miteinander kombiniert werden. Die Themen sind dabei schülernah, da sie in vielen Fällen zum Vergleich der Erfahrungswelt der Lernenden mit dem jeweiligen Zielland anregen. Dadurch wird die Bereitschaft der Schüler sich mitzuteilen gestärkt und sie werden zu einer Auseinandersetzung mit der eigenen Kultur und der Kultur Großbritanniens angeregt. Gleichzeitig finden sich auch historische Themen – wie zum Beispiel eine erste Begegnung mit *William Shakespeare* und dem *Globe Theatre* – in diesem Band wieder, die gerade für geschichtsbegeisterte Lerngruppen gedacht sind.

An die 40 Kopiervorlagen schließen sich detaillierte didaktisch-methodische Hinweise samt Lösungsvorschlägen zu allen Kopiervorlagen an. Die meisten Arbeitsblätter sind für eine 45-minütige Unterrichtsstunde konzipiert – sollte mehr Zeit benötigt werden, findet sich eine entsprechende Zeitangabe im Kommentar zur Kopiervorlage. Darüber hinaus werden für viele Arbeitsblätter Alternativen und Möglichkeiten der Binnendifferenzierung vorgeschlagen. Zu einigen Differenzierungsmöglichkeiten bietet dieser Band zudem abrufbares Zusatzmaterial an, so dass die Lehrkraft die Kopiervorlage optimal an die Lerngruppe anpassen kann. Weitere Zusatzmaterialien (Audio-Dateien, Links zu Videos, Kopiervorlagen) stehen ebenfalls für die Lehrkraft zum Download bereit.

Abkürzungen und Symbole:

💬	Sprechen
📖	Lesen
✏️	Schreiben
🎧	Hör-/Sehverstehen
SuS	Schülerinnen und Schüler
KV	Kopiervorlage
👥	Partnerarbeit
👨‍👩‍👧	Gruppenarbeit/Plenum
💭	Sprachmittlung, Mediationsaufgabe
🏠	Hausaufgabe
📕	Wörterbuch
🌐	Zusatzmaterialien online
▲	Differenzierung

🌐 **Zusatzmaterialien online**
Geben Sie bitte den Code **7p6pk3b** in das Suchfeld auf www.klett-sprachen.de ein. Sie gelangen dann zu einer Internetseite mit weiteren Materialien und Links zu dieser Lehrerhandreichung.

1 Customs and traditions: special events

British Christmas traditions

1. How do you celebrate Christmas at home? Think of some Christmas traditions and share them with your partner. If you don't celebrate Christmas think of winter traditions instead.

2. Read the role profiles below and make sure you know the words in English. Get together in small groups and choose one role profile each. Then imagine the following situation: Dennis and Anna are on an exchange trip to London and there is a big Christmas concert at a school. In the break Dennis and Anna start talking to Ben, Maliha and Amar (who only speak English) about different Christmas traditions in Germany and Great Britain. Act out the situation in your group.

Role profiles:

Maliha: 13 years old, lives in London, family from Pakistan, Muslim

Traditions:
- 25th December: big family meal (turkey, roast potatoes…)
- no presents but a lot of time to play games with siblings and other relatives

Ben: 13 years old, from London, Christian

Traditions:
- sing Christmas carols (*Rudolph the red-nosed reindeer, Jingle bells*)
- hang Christmas stockings over the fireplace
- open presents early in the morning on Christmas Day (25th December)
- eat Christmas dinner with family (turkey or goose, potatoes, brussel sprouts…)

Dennis: 13 Jahre alt, aus Stuttgart, Christ

Traditionen:
- auf Weihnachtsmarkt gehen (Glühpunsch trinken und rote Wurst essen)
- Schlittschuhlaufen
- Krippe aufstellen
- 24.12. nachmittags in die Kirche; abends mit Familie essen (Würstchen & Kartoffelsalat), dann Geschenke öffnen, Lieder singen

Anna: 12 Jahre alt, aus Hannover

Traditionen:
- Tannenbaum kaufen und gemeinsam mit der Schwester schmücken
- Weihnachtsplätzchen backen und verzieren
- 24.12. nachmittags Geschenke auspacken und abends in die Christmette
- 25.12. großes Familienessen (Weihnachtsgans)

Amar: 12 years old, lives in London, family from India, Hindu

Traditions:
- celebrate *Pancha Ganapati* (a modern Hindu festival from 21st to 25th December)
- decorate a statue of Lord Ganapati with green pine branches and blinking lights
- every day the children dress the statue in a different colour (yellow, blue, red, green, orange)
- children get presents each day and open them on 25th December

3. These are a lot of different traditions! If you could choose between the German and British Christmas traditions, which would you like better? Which do you find interesting? Which one would you like to find out more about? Talk to your partner about these questions.

Guy Fawkes

1. Read the two texts about Guy Fawkes.

Historical background

Text 1

On 5th November 1605 a man called Guy Fawkes wanted to blow up the Houses of Parliament in London and kill the King of England, James I. Who was the man behind this attack?

Guy Fawkes was born in 1570 in Stonegate, York. His family was Protestant because this was the official religion in England but secretly they were Catholic and Guy Fawkes also became a Catholic when he was
5 a teenager. He became a soldier and left England to fight for Catholic countries like Spain against Protestant countries like the Netherlands. During this time he learned how to use gunpowder[1]. When he came back to England, Guy Fawkes and his partners, who were also all Catholics, wanted to kill James I. The reason for this plan was that they thought that Catholics were discriminated against in England because the former Queen, Elizabeth I, had passed some unfair laws against the Catholics. Guy Fawkes
10 hid[2] gunpowder in the basement of the Houses of Parliament but he was discovered before he could light the fuse[3] and the attack was stopped. He was then taken to the Tower of London where he confessed[4] the names of his partners and they were all sentenced to death[5].

1 **gunpowder** *Schießpulver* – 2 **(to) hide (hid, hidden)** *verstecken* – 3 **(to) light the fuse** *die Zündschnur anzünden* –
4 **(to) confess sth** *etw gestehen* – 5 **(to) be sentenced to sth** *zu etw verurteilt werden*

Remembering Guy Fawkes

Text 2

Today, 5th November is a special day in Britain. People light huge bonfires[1] and they burn Guy Fawkes dummies[2] (called "guys"). There are also fireworks to celebrate King James I having survived the *Gunpowder Plot*[3] in 1605. This day is often
5 called *Guy Fawkes Day*, also known as *Bonfire Night* and *Guy Fawkes Night*.

1 **bonfire** *Freudenfeuer* – 2 **dummy** *Puppe, Attrappe* –
3 **the Gunpowder Plot** *die Pulververschwörung*

2. Tick true or false. Write down the text number and the line(s) where you found the information.

	true	false	text	line(s)
a) Guy Fawkes was born in 1570.	☐	☐	_____	_____
b) Guy Fawkes was a Protestant when he was a teenager.	☐	☐	_____	_____
c) Guy Fawkes used gunpowder when he was a soldier.	☐	☐	_____	_____
d) Together with some friends Guy Fawkes wanted to murder the king.	☐	☐	_____	_____
e) Guy Fawkes had to live in the Tower of London for the rest of his life.	☐	☐	_____	_____
f) People burn Guy Fawkes dummies on 5th November every year.	☐	☐	_____	_____
g) 5th November is known as Guy Fawkes Day.	☐	☐	_____	_____

3. Make your own Guy Fawkes quiz. Write five new questions in your exercise book. Then swap with a partner and answer their questions. You can find out more about Guy Fawkes on the Internet. Do some research on your own or ask your teacher for some links.

3 Customs and traditions: special events

SPOOKY HALLOWEEN

1. What do you know about Halloween? Write down the things you know already. You can do this as a mind map or simply as a list.

2. Compare what you know about Halloween with the information from the text. Add the new information to your mind map. Which aspects do you find most interesting?

> Halloween is a special event which takes place on the evening of 31st October. In the beginning, over 2000 years ago, it was a Celtic and Pagan tradition. The people then had a different calendar and 31st October was the last day of summer. The Celts celebrated the end of summer and the beginning of winter with big fires. They also believed that the ghosts of dead people would come back during the night and be with their families and friends. But some ghosts did not have families and friends to visit and they haunted[1] and scared other people. Later, the 1st of November, the day after Halloween, became a Catholic holiday to remember all dead people. Today Halloween is celebrated all over the world and especially in the USA. Children dress up in scary costumes like witches or monsters and walk around their neighbourhood to collect sweets. This is called *trick or treat* because they stop at a house and ask the people who live there for a *treat* like sweets. If the children don't get any sweets, they will play a *trick* on them, for example, put toilet paper everywhere or scare them. Another tradition is a *Jack O'Lantern*. It's a pumpkin with a carved face and a candle inside. People put it on their doorstep to remember an Irish man called *Stingy Jack*[2] who made a pact with the devil. The *Jack O'Lantern* is one of the most well-known Halloween symbols in the world. Have you ever made one?
>
> 1 **to haunt sb** *when a ghosts visits and scares you, it haunts you*
> 2 **stingy** *if you don't want to spend any money because you want to keep it all for yourself, you're stingy*

3. With all this Halloween information you are now an expert! Write a scary Halloween story in your exercise book or on a piece of paper. Use as many scary adjectives from the language box below as you can. Check the words in a dictionary.

Language box – A–Z Halloween adjectives

> **a**larming, **b**loody, **c**reepy, **d**readful, **e**erie, **f**rightening, **g**hostly, **h**orrifying, **i**ntimidating, **j**ittery, **k**illing, **l**urking, **m**ad, **n**asty, **o**bnoxious, **p**anicky, **q**uerulous, **r**otten, **s**pooky, **t**errifying, **u**nbearable, **v**ile, **w**eird, **a**nxious, **y**ucky, **z**any

When you have finished, let your classmates read your story and get them to do the following **spookiness ranking**. On a scale of 1 to 10: How spooky is this story? Circle the number.

Yawn! Not spooky at all!   1   2   3   4   5   6   7   8   9   10   *Aaaaargh! Super spooky!*

Merry Christmas!

1. What do you know about Christmas traditions in Germany and the UK? Write down the things you know already. You can write key words.

Christmas traditions in Germany	Christmas traditions in the UK

2. Let's find out more about Christmas traditions in the UK.

   a) Watch the video and decide whether the sentences are true or false. Correct the wrong sentences.

	true	false
1. You can go ice-skating at Christmas.	☐	☐
2. There are no Christmas markets in the UK.	☐	☐
3. People in the UK don't buy Christmas presents for their family.	☐	☐
4. People in the UK decorate their Christmas tree.	☐	☐

   _____

   _____

   _____

   b) Watch the video again and complete the sentences of Ashlie and Stephen.

   Stephen: Ashlie and I are supposed to be doing some last-minute _____.

   Ashlie: We're cooking _____ for the _____ this year.

   Stephen: And we've still got lots of _____ to buy.

   Stephen: I love _____, Ash. It's so exciting!

   Ashlie: I know! All the _____, the wonderful _____. I can't wait!

   Ashlie: Come on, let's _____ _____ our stockings.

   Stephen: Ok. They look great. And look, I've put out some mince pies for when _____ Christmas comes down the chimney and some _____ for the reindeer.

3. Look at the table from task 1 and fill in missing traditions that you found out about in the video. Write down what you find funny or strange and why. Also write down which Christmas tradition you would like to know more about.

British food

1. Talk about your favourite food: What do you eat for breakfast, lunch and dinner? If you don't know all the names in English, paraphrase them.

2. The pictures of British meals below were taken by foodies. Identify the food and compare them with your typical meals. Write down the similarities and differences.

3. Prepare a short presentation on the differences between your food and the British meals. If you lived in Britain, which German food would you miss most? Which British food would you like to try? Explain your answers.

> **foodie** a person who enjoys and cares about food very much; a food-loving person; foodies often take pictures of their food and share them with other people

1

2

3

4

5

6

Customs and traditions: food and drinks

Tea Time

Tea – past and present

There is almost nothing as British as a nice hot cup of tea, and it has been this way for a long time. This is a bit strange because tea plants do not grow in Britain – the climate is too cold. But why is tea still a typically British beverage[1]?

5 In the past, about 350 years ago, Britain bought tea from China but it was very expensive[2]. Only rich people could afford[3] it. At that time Britain controlled countries all over the world (these countries are called colonies) and it was called the *British Empire*[4]. India was one of these colonies and it was possible to grow tea there. In Assam, a region in India, the first Indian tea was produced and *Assam tea* is still popular today.

10 Because India is closer to Britain than China, it was much cheaper to bring tea to Britain from there. One of the fastest ships which brought tea from India is the *Cutty Sark*. Today it is a museum ship and you can visit it in Greenwich, south-east London.

When the prices for tea dropped, more people in Britain were able to buy and drink tea and many new *tea houses* were opened. But tea was not only sold in Britain. The *East India Company*, a British trading company[5], sold tea to all

15 parts of the world. The connection between Britain and tea spread[6].

There are some well-known traditions for tea drinking: When you are invited for *afternoon tea* you usually drink tea and eat cold snacks such as small sandwiches and cakes in the afternoon. There is also a short break during the morning at about 11 a.m. called *Elevenses*, when you drink tea and eat biscuits. People usually drink their tea with a little milk and sometimes sugar.

20 However, nowadays more and more people drink coffee and there are coffee shops everywhere. Will tea still be so popular in the future? We will see.

1 **beverage** a drink – 2 **expensive** when sth costs a lot of money – 3 **(to) afford sth** sich etw leisten können – 4 **the British Empire** das Britische Weltreich – 5 **trading company** Handelsgesellschaft – 6 **(to) spread** sich verbreiten

---

1. Read the text about the importance of tea in Britain.

2. Tick true or false. Write down the line(s) where you found the information.

	true	false	line(s)
a) Tea is typically British.	☐	☐	_____
b) The weather in Britain is perfect for tea plants.	☐	☐	_____
c) At first, all the tea came from China.	☐	☐	_____
d) Tea was brought to Britain by train.	☐	☐	_____
e) People couldn't afford tea from India.	☐	☐	_____
f) The morning break for tea is known as *Tenses*.	☐	☐	_____
g) Most people in Britain add milk to their tea.	☐	☐	_____

3. Complete the sentences in your OWN words. Write the sentences into your exercise book.

   a) It was possible to grow tea in India because …
   b) Tea is typically British because …
   c) Today people in Britain drink …

4. Are you a tea drinker? Which kind of tea do you like? Who would you invite for a tea party? Which tea tradition would you create? Think about these questions and share your ideas with a partner.

7 Customs and traditions: food and drinks

A British recipe[1] – Shepherd's Pie[2]

1. How often do you cook or bake? What meals can you cook? Talk about this with a partner.

2. Read the recipe of this typical British dish[3]. There are a lot of very specific words and you probably won't know them all. Make a list of all the words you don't know and look them up in a dictionary.

Shepherd's Pie

Ingredients (serves 6)

2 Tbsp olive oil * 2 carrots * 500 g minced meat (lamb or beef)

1 red onion * 1 clove of garlic * a small bunch of fresh rosemary

salt * pepper * 1 tin of chopped tomatoes

1.5 kg potatoes * 100 ml milk * green peas (fresh or frozen)

250 ml vegetable stock * butter

Preparation

Peel and chop the onion, the garlic clove, the carrots and the rosemary leaves.

Heat a large pan on a medium heat, add the olive oil, onion, garlic, carrot and rosemary and stir them until they are soft. Turn up the heat and add the minced meat. Brown it for 10 minutes and stir from time to time. Then pour in the tomatoes and the stock. Add some salt and pepper and bring it to the boil. Reduce the heat and let it simmer for 1 hour.

Peel the potatoes, cut them and boil them in water for about ten minutes until they are cooked. Drain them in a colander and put them back in the pan. Add milk, butter and a pinch of salt and pepper. Mash them until soft and creamy.

Preheat the oven to 190°C. Pour the meat mixture in an ovenproof baking dish and place the mashed potatoes on top. Cook in the oven for about 25 minutes.

Enjoy your meal!

Tip
Serve with cooked peas.

Are you hungry yet? ☺

2. Imagine your exchange student from Bristol asks you for a typical German dish. Choose a recipe – it can be something to cook or something to bake. Write the ingredients and instructions in English for your friend. Find or draw a picture to put next to your recipe. You can even create an international cookbook with your class and try out new recipes.

---

1 **recipe** ['resıpi] *Rezept* – 2 **Shepherd's Pie** *Auflauf aus Hackfleisch und Kartoffelbrei* – 3 **dish** *Gericht*

Customs and traditions: food and drinks   8

British food culture

1. What do you know about British food? Write the things you know already in a mind map.

(British food)

2. Let's find out more about food in Britain.

   a) Watch the video and tick (✓) the correct answer.

   Who introduced oriental food to Britain?
   ☐ the Italians   ☐ the French   ☐ the Chinese

   Borough Market is …
   ☐ a supermarket.   ☐ London's oldest food market.   ☐ London's biggest market.

   This is not part of a full English breakfast:
   ☐ tomato   ☐ bacon   ☐ cheese

   Celia Brooks Brown is a …
   ☐ chef[1]   ☐ food writer   ☐ waitress[2]

   b) Watch the video again and complete the sentences.

   1. _____ from all around the _____ can be found on most British high streets.

   2. A big fried _____ might not be to everyone's taste. But in Britain, there is something for _____.

   3. People want to know _____ their food comes _____.

   4. Chefs love to experiment with ingredients[3] from _____ _____.

3. Look at the mind map from task 1 and fill in new information that you found out about in the video. Explain why British chefs are reinventing[4] classic British dishes[5].

4. Campaign: Promoting British food! Create a poster which tells people that the stereotype "British food is bad" is not true anymore.

   Extra: Find out where you can buy British food in your area. Ask your parents if you can cook a typical British dish. Maybe you can meet with friends and cook together.

---

1 **chef** Koch – 2 **waitress** Kellnerin, Bedienung – 3 **ingredient** Zutat – 4 **(to) reinvent sth** etw neu erfinden – 5 **dish** Gericht

History: people

Growing up royal

1. The British royal family is one of the most famous families in the world. You will probably know many of its members. Fill in the family tree of the royal family: Prince Edward – Prince Harry – Prince Philip – Princess Anne – Prince Andrew – Princess Diana – Princess Charlotte – Camilla, Duchess of Cornwall – Princess Catherine – Prince George.

2. Get together with a partner. One of you is partner A, the other partner B. Explain how the following members of the family are related:

   partner A: 1) Prince George – Prince Charles   2) Prince Philip – Prince Edward   3) Princess Charlotte – the Queen
   partner B: 1) Camilla – Prince Harry   2) Prince William – Prince Andrew   3) Princess Anne – Prince Philip

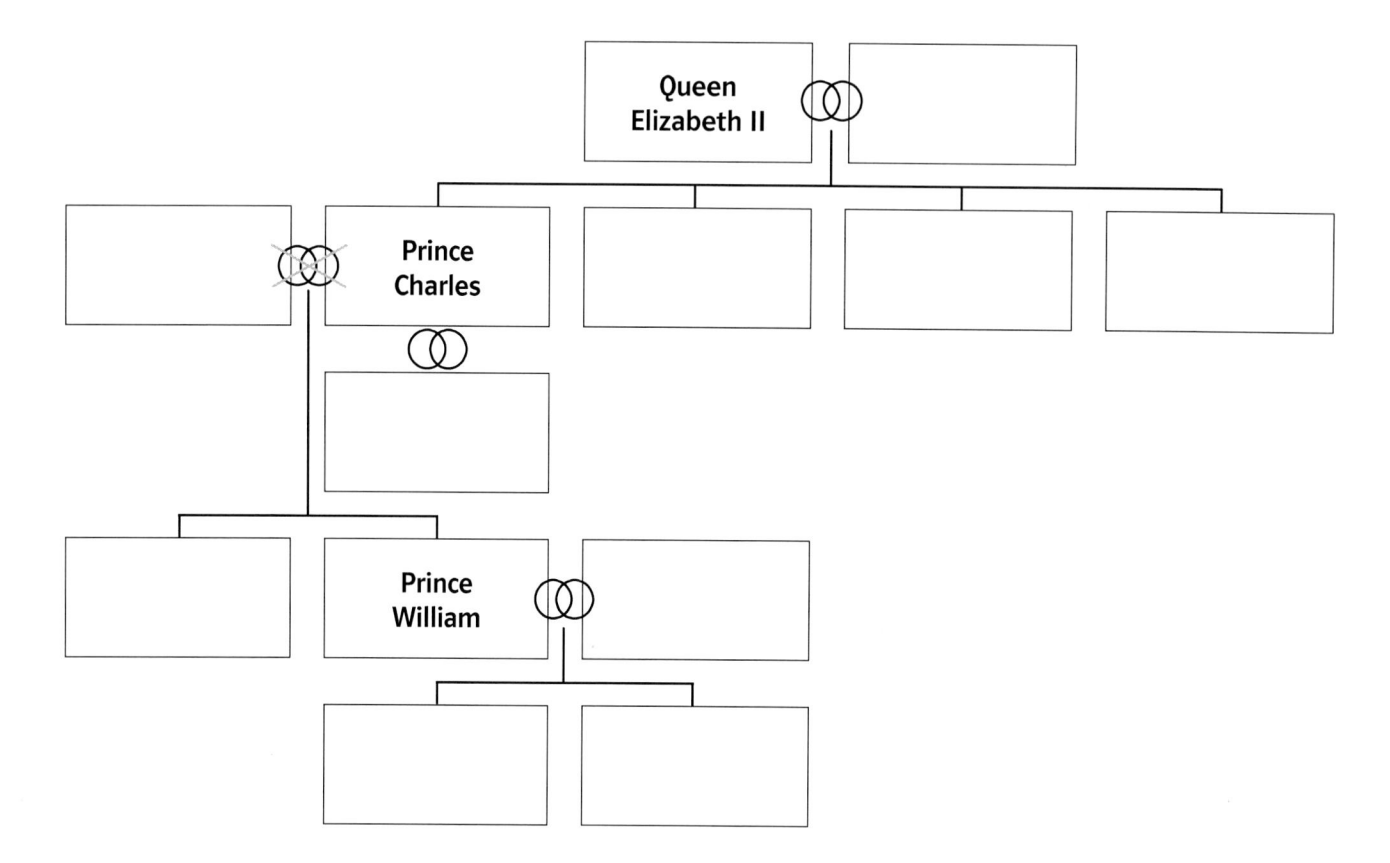

3. Prince George is the oldest son of William and Catherine (Kate). His childhood is different from yours. Get together in groups. Think of what is good and bad about growing up as a royal. Copy the grid into your exercise book.

☺ advantages of growing up royal	☹ disadvantages of growing up royal

4. Put yourself in Prince George's shoes. Would you like to grow up like him? Look at the useful phrases and say why (not).

   I would prefer (not) to … because …
   I (don't) like about being royal that …
   The biggest (dis)advantage of being royal is …
   If I were a prince/princess, I would …

William Shakespeare – a world-famous writer

1. What is your favourite book? Who is your favourite author? Talk about them in class.
2. One of the most famous writers in the world is William Shakespeare. Read the text about his life and then answer the questions below.

Though William Shakespeare is one of the most famous writers in the world, nobody knows when he was born. He was baptised[1] in Stratford-upon-Avon, England, on 26 April 1564. Some people believe he was born two days before. His father John was a glove-maker[2] and an important man in town. He sent
5 Shakespeare to grammar school[3] where he learned Latin. He left school at the age of 16. Two years later he married Anne Hathaway, who was 8 years older than him. They had a daughter (Susanna) and twins (Judith and Hamnet).

It is not known what Shakespeare did for a living at that time. He may have worked as a teacher for rich families. Around 1590 he went to London – without his family. There he became an actor[4] and part of a
10 group called *The Lord Chamberlain's Men*. In 1598, they built a new theatre near the Thames. They called it the "Globe".

Eventually Shakespeare became a famous playwright[5], too. He wrote 39 plays in his lifetime. Some of them were comedies, stories with a happy ending, like *A Midsummer Night's Dream*. Some of them were tragedies, stories with a sad ending, like his most famous play *Romeo and Juliet*.

15 In 1613 the Globe burned down and Shakespeare left London to live a quiet life with his family. He died on 23 April 1616.

Although Shakespeare has been dead for about 400 years, people still go to see his plays. They are performed[5] all over the world, for example in the new *Globe Theatre* in London. Pupils and students study Shakespeare's work at school and university.

1 **baptised** *getauft* – 2 **glove** *Handschuh* – 3 **grammar school** *Lateinschule* – 4 **actor** *Schauspieler* – 5 **playwright** *Dramatiker* – 6 **to perform** *aufführen*

---

3. Write the questions and your answers into your exercise book. Write down the line(s) where you found the information.

    a) When was Shakespeare born?
    b) Where did Shakespeare learn Latin?
    c) How old was he when he got married?
    d) What did Shakespeare do for a living?
    e) Where did the *Chamberlain's Men* build the *Globe*?
    f) What is the title of Shakespeare's most popular tragedy?
    g) How old was Shakespeare when he died in 1616?

4. Have a guess: Which of these fun facts about William Shakespeare are true? Talk to your partner.

    true (✓)

    a) In his will[7] Shakespeare left his wife "the second-best bed". ☐
    b) "Shakespeare" was spelled 80 different ways, e.g. *Shaxpere* and *Shaxberd*. ☐
    c) About the time Shakespeare was born the first pen was invented[8]. ☐
    d) Shakespeare played the ghost in his famous play *Hamlet*. ☐
    e) Shakespeare introduced almost 3,000 words into the English language, for example *bedroom* and *eyeball*. ☐
    f) His mother called him "Willy". ☐

7 **will** *Testament* – 8 **to invent** *erfinden*

Conversation with a Viking

1. *What does a Viking look like? Draw a Viking and compare your picture with your partner's.*

2. *Read what Harold the Viking tells you about his life. He would like to get to know you, too. Answer his questions.*

Harold: *Hej*! I'm Harold, son of Cnut the Great, the first Viking to become King of England. Nice to meet you. What's your name?

You: _____

Harold: That's a name I've never heard before! Where are you from?

You: _____

Harold: I live in England, but my family comes from Denmark. We are Vikings and my father Cnut took over England the year I was born. Next year, in 1030, I'll be fifteen which means I'll be an adult – a real Viking! I can't wait! My biggest dream is to be king one day, just like my father. How old are you and what would you like to do when you're a grown-up?

You: _____

Harold: That's interesting! I've never heard of anything like that. Most of my friends want to become raiders. That means they want to go to another country in a longship and take away goods from other people. I'm more interested in hunting. My friends call me *Harefoot* because I'm as fast as a rabbit. I also like to swim and wrestle. What activities do you like?

You: _____

Harold: My favourite game is *hnefatafl* which means *king's table* in English. It's a game where you move pieces around a board. I also like to sit around the fireplace and listen to sagas about elves and trolls. What kind of stories do you like?

You: _____

Harold: I would really like to hear more about your stories. But I'm afraid I have to leave you for now. My father wants me to go on a hunting trip with him. *Far vel!*

3. *Choose a partner and act out the conversation.*

4. *"Saga", "elves" and "trolls" are old Viking words which are used in English today. Find five more English words with a Viking background on the Internet. Share them with your class.*

History: people   12

Sherlock Holmes – Mrs Hudson's lucky day

1. The author Sir Arthur Conan Doyle is famous for his stories about London's well-known detective Sherlock Holmes. Sherlock Holmes is very clever and lives at 221B Baker Street. His landlady Mrs Hudson lives in the same house. But one day Mrs Hudson goes missing! Can you help Sherlock Holmes to find out what had happened to her? Listen to the famous detective. Answer the questions.

   a) Who phoned Sherlock Holmes yesterday? What did the person tell him?

   _____

   b) When did Sherlock Holmes last see Mrs Hudson?

   _____

   c) How was the weather the day Mrs Hudson visited Mrs Spencer and what did she take with her?

   _____

   d) What did Mrs Hudson do at Mrs Spencer's house?

   _____

   e) What did Mrs Hudson say when she left Mrs Spencer?

   _____

2. Look at the picture of Mrs Hudson's kitchen table. Draw a circle around the things which can help you to solve the case. Then explain what happened to Mrs Hudson.

3. What would you do if you were Mrs Hudson? Write down your ideas.

History: places

A guided tour of the Tower of London

1. Look at London's skyline. Which London sights can you see? Which would you like to visit and why? Talk about it with your partner.

2. You are taking a guided tour of the Tower of London with your parents. Your parents' English isn't good enough to understand your tour guide. Mediate between your tour guide and parents.
   Get together in groups of three and act out the dialogue. Do this three times, so that everyone plays each role once.

   Guide Good morning, ladies and gentlemen. Welcome to Her Majesty's Royal Palace[1] and Fortress[2], known as the Tower of London. For the next hour I'm your guide. Please stay close to me and follow me as we start our tour.

   You ...

   Parent Kannst du ihn bitte fragen, ob man während der Tour Fotos machen kann?

   You ...

   Guide Yes, of course you can. But don't take too many pictures of me!

   You ...

   Guide The Tower of London has been a palace and fortress for nearly a thousand years. It was never just a prison[3]. Well, we had about 3,500 prisoners here, too, but there is much more to this place.

   You ...

   Guide For example, the Crown Jewels[4] of the United Kingdom have been kept in the Tower of London since 1303. Queen Elizabeth only wears them at ceremonies, most of the time they are stored[5] in the Jewel House. They are the main attraction. Look! Can you see the people queuing[6]?

   You ...

   Parent Oh, das sind ja viele Menschen! Wie viele Besucher kommen denn jedes Jahr hierher?

   You ...

   Guide Well, each year about 3 million people from all over the world come to visit the Tower of London. The Tower is one of the tourists' favourite sights.

   You ...

   Parent Und wie lange muss man anstehen, um die Kronjuwelen zu sehen?

   You ...

   Guide On busy days like today you have to wait for more than an hour to see the Crown Jewels.

   You ...

   Parent Das ist aber ganz schön lang! Sollen wir das wirklich machen, was meinst du?

   1 **palace** *Palast, Schloss* – 2 **fortress** *Festung, Feste* – 3 **prison** *Gefängnis* – 4 **Crown Jewels** *Kronjuwelen* – 5 **stored** *aufbewahrt* – 6 **to queue** *anstehen*

3. Would you wait one hour or more to see the Crown Jewels? Say why (not).

Stonehenge of Scotland

1. Read the text. Then draw a sketch of the Standing Stones of Callanish seen from a bird's-eye view in your exercise book.

The *Isle of Lewis* is one of the loneliest places in Scotland. Only 18,000 people live on the island. But you can find one of the oldest stone circles there, which is as old as the Egyptian[1] pyramids and older than Stonehenge in England. That's why it is also called the "Stonehenge of Scotland".

In 1844 Sir James Matheson, a rich Scotsman, bought the *Isle of Lewis* for £ 190,000. He didn't know about the old and long forgotten history of this island.

At that time, peat[2] was used for fuel[3] by the people of the island. By 1857 much of the peat near the village of Calanais had been used. When Sir Matheson had the last peat taken away, a long forgotten stone circle was found in the ground. Today the *Standing Stones of Callanish* are known as one of the oldest stone circles in Europe.

Experts say the stone circle was built around 3000 BC. At first, there were only 13 stones in a circle around a bigger central stone, which is 4.8 metres high and weighs[4] about seven tonnes. About 1000 years later two rows of stones were added[5]. The rows connect to the stone circle from the north. They consist of[6] 19 stones (nine on the eastern side, ten on the western side).

There are other stones connecting to the stone circle in a row (four in the west, five in the east, seven in the south). Together with the row in the north they form a cross. Between the central stone and the eastern stones there is a cairn[7] which was built later than the stones.

Many experts tried to find out why the *Standing Stones of Callanish* were built, but their function is still unknown. It is said that the stones were a moon calendar. The rest of their history is a mystery[8]. Maybe this is the reason why around 40,000 tourists come to visit the *Callanish Standing Stones* each year.

1 **Egyptian** ägyptisch – 2 **peat** Torf – 3 **fuel** Brennstoff – 4 **to weigh** wiegen – 5 **to add** hinzufügen – 6 **to consist of** bestehen aus – 7 **cairn** Hügelgrab – 8 **mystery** Rätsel

2. Compare the Standing Stones of Callanish with Stonehenge. Use the information from the text as well as the following information on Stonehenge:

- in Wiltshire, England
- built between 2400 and 2200 BC
- 79 stones
- stones: up to nine metres high
- one million visitors per year

… than …
more … than …
(not) as … as …
the most …

3. Compare the Standing Stones of Callanish with a tourist attraction in your hometown. Collect information on your hometown's tourist attraction and then write about these two tourist attractions.

History: places

Romans in Britain – Life on Hadrian's Wall

1. Look at the picture. Describe the two men.
   - Who are they?
   - Where are they from?
   - What are they doing?

   Talk about it in class.

2. The men are soldiers on Hadrian's Wall. Read the text to find out when and why they came to Britain.

   Did you know that Julius Caesar, the famous Roman general, came to Britain twice?
   In 55 BC he led his army across the Channel from France to Britain. He wanted to make
   5 Britain part of the Roman Empire[1]. Therefore he started a war against the people who lived there, the Celts[2]. But the Celts fought back bravely and won. Caesar had to leave Britain. He came back a year later with a bigger
   10 army – but he failed again to invade[3] Britain and left forever.

   For about one hundred years no more Romans were seen in Britain. In 43 AD the Romans returned, though. Emperor Claudius sent an army to invade Britain. This time the Romans were successful[4] and made the southern half of Britain part of the Roman Empire. The Roman soldiers stayed in Britain for
   15 hundreds of years.

   After they had conquered[5] Britain the Romans had to defend their new territory[6]. In 122 AD the Emperor Hadrian built a wall between Britain and Scotland, because Scotland didn't belong to the Romans. The wall was 117 km long and ran from Wallsend in the east to Bowness on the Solway Firth. You can still walk along parts of Hadrian's Wall today.

   20 Life on Hadrian's Wall was hard for the soldiers who guarded[7] the border[8]. Most of them were not used to the Scottish weather because they came from all parts of Europe like Spain, France and Italy. Some of them had never seen snow before! In addition, up to ten soldiers had to live in one barrack together with their horses. Sometimes the soldiers were homesick because they were far away from home. But there was a good side to the life on Hadrian's Wall, too: The soldiers traded[9] food and goods with the Scottish
   25 people and a lot of the soldiers married women from the other side of the wall. And there were bathhouses, so soldiers could take a bath after their watch.

   1 **empire** Reich – 2 **Celts** Kelten – 3 **(to) invade** überfallen – 4 **sucessful** erfolgreich – 5 **to conquer** erobern – 6 **territory** Gebiet – 7 **(to) guard** bewachen – 8 **border** Grenze – 9 **(to) trade** handeln

3. Imagine you are a soldier at Hadrian's Wall. Write a letter to your family about your life at the wall.

History: places   16

Shakespeare's Globe

1. Do you like to go to the theatre? Have you ever been in a play? Talk about it in class.

2. One of the most popular tourist attractions in London is Shakespeare's Globe. It's not the original theatre from Shakespeare's time but a modern version. Look at the picture of Shakespeare's Globe. Describe what you can see in the picture. How is the Globe different from theatres you know?

Labels on picture: the hut, upper stage, main stage, trap door, pit, gallery (lower, middle, upper)

3. Let's find out more about the Globe. Watch the video and decide whether the sentences are true or false.

		true	false
a)	The Globe is the theatre where Shakespeare's plays were first performed in London.	☐	☐
b)	The first Globe theatre was built in the 16th century.	☐	☐
c)	The modern Globe theatre was built in the same place as the first Globe.	☐	☐
d)	Shakespeare was one of the owners of the first Globe.	☐	☐
e)	The first Globe theatre burnt down during the Great Fire of London.	☐	☐
f)	Men and women acted out the plays.	☐	☐

4. Watch the video again. Correct the wrong sentences in task 3.

5. Do an Internet research on Shakespeare's Globe in London: Where in London is it? What does it look like inside? When can you go there? Can you take a guided tour? How much is the entrance fee?
Write a text about Shakespeare's Globe into your exercise book. You can attach a photo to it if you like.

School uniforms – a necessary evil?

Useful words

blouse / shirt • jacket • pullover / sweater • skirt • (pair of) trousers / jeans • socks • short / long • pretty / cool / boring • casual / smart • fashionable / colourful / plaid[1] • today I'm wearing • my favourite clothes

1. Describe the pictures. Who is from Great Britain and who is from Germany?

2. Pros and cons of wearing school uniforms: Get together with a partner and find arguments for and against school uniforms. Collect your ideas in a list and then discuss them in class. Add new pros and cons to your list.

Pro uniforms	Against uniforms
no bullying, less time needed to get ready in the morning	uncomfortable, no individuality

3. Choose one:
   a) Design your ideal school uniform. Think about the disadvantages in your list.
   b) Teachers should also wear some kind of uniform: Design a uniform for teachers.

   Here are some things you should keep in mind:

   - Think about the rules for hairstyles.
   - What about items like mobile phones, bags, hats, jewellery etc?
   - Should there be a rule for make-up?
   - Think about different cultures and religions.

   c) Present your design in class, e.g. on a poster. You can add drawings or photos.

4. Would you like to have school uniforms at your school? Why/Why not?

5. Sanctions[2]:

   "An eight-year-old boy has been suspended[3] from school for turning up to lessons with a shaved head."

   What if a student breaks the school's dress code? What kind of sanctions should be imposed[4]? Can you agree on fair sanctions?

1 **plaid** *kariert* – 2 **sanction** *Strafmaßnahme* – 3 **suspend** *ausschließen* – 4 **impose** *auferlegen, verhängen*

Sean's day at school

Sean is a student at an English grammar school. Here's his letter to his German penfriend Thomas:

Hi Thomas,   27th June, 2016

it's good to hear from you. I really enjoyed reading about your family and hobbies. You wanted to know about my school in Birmingham. Well, let me describe it to you.

I go to Handsworth Grammar School: a school for boys only. A typical school day starts very early: I usually leave home at 6:45 and walk 20 minutes to the bus stop. The school bus only picks up students from my school. It takes about an hour to get to school because we have to stop regularly on the way. On the bus, my friends and I chat all the way to school. On Mondays we are usually tired but happy to see each other. When we arrive at school, I go to my tutor room for registration at 8:30.

Each subject is in a different room, so I usually have to go to a different room for each lesson. All rooms have a number or a name. I also have different teachers for each subject.

We are a very modern school. Every student has a swipe card. The card has two stripes: a black one and a brown one. We use it to swipe into lessons so the school knows we've gone to the lesson. It's also helpful to know where every student is e.g. in case of an emergency. The black stripe allows us access to toilets and other rooms in the school building. The cards are also used to pay at the cafeteria. We don't use cash. Of course, you have to put credit on the card first! I really love our swipe cards.

There is a 20-minute break before the third period starts and another 10-minute break after the third period. During the short break, I have a snack and play and chat with my friends. Usually we play hide and seek.

I'm always very hungry at lunch time. Sometimes my mom gives me a packed lunch, but I prefer to go to the cafeteria. There, my friends and I have spaghetti or just some chips. At ten past two I have to be back for my last period. School is over at ten past three.

So, what about your German school? Is it like mine? What's different? I am looking forward to your next letter.

Yours, Sean

1. Read the text and tick the correct answers.

   Sean's trip to school is
   - [ ] 60 minutes long.
   - [ ] fun.
   - [ ] 20 minutes long.
   - [ ] boring.

   Swipe cards are great because you can
   - [ ] put credit on them.
   - [ ] go home when you want.
   - [ ] save your homework.
   - [ ] get into rooms.

   How many breaks does Sean have at school every day?
   - [ ] two
   - [ ] only lunch break
   - [ ] four
   - [ ] three

2. Read the text and give the correct answer.

   Where does Sean meet his friends first every day? _____

   How long is Sean's school day? _____

   What can you eat at the cafeteria? _____

3. Write an e-mail to Sean and tell him about your school and a typical school day.

4. Make a table: a day at your German school and a day at Sean's English school.

19 School and beyond

A school trip to the Isle of Wight

1. Find the Isle of Wight on a map of Great Britain. Describe where it is.

2. You're visiting your penfriend Celia/Tim who lives in Portsmouth. One day, her/his class goes on a school trip to the Isle of Wight. You go with them. Write an e-mail to your English class at home about what you have seen and done on the island. Use your notes and the photos below as a help.

- Monkey Haven
- see, feed, play with monkeys
- not only a zoo: care for animals in need
- public feeding once a day
- fantastic time
- a gibbon stole Celia's/Tim's sandwich

- Osborne House
- Queen Victoria's summer home
- Swiss Cottage (originally a cottage in Switzerland brought piece by piece to Osborne) with its own gardens for the royal children
- Prince Albert's Dressing Room
- beautiful and big, but a bit boring (teachers: very excited)

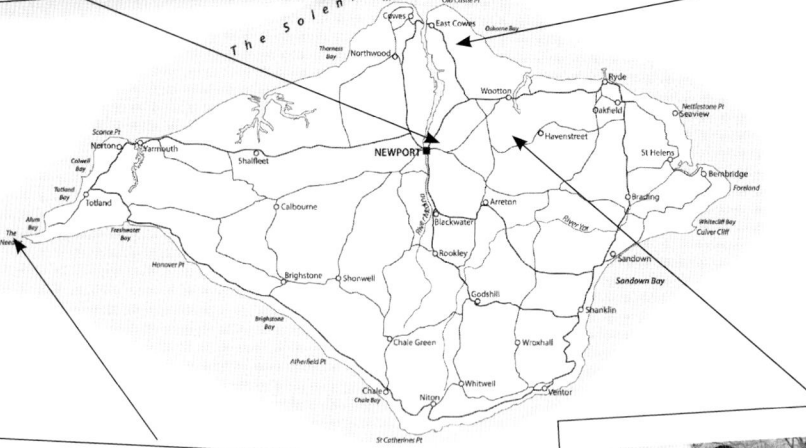

- Needles Rocks
- three chalk rocks, so very white
- name comes from fourth rock which looked like a needle (it's not there anymore)
- all the tourists go there, most famous sight on the island
- took a windy boat trip

- Steam Railway
- watch the island's beautiful nature
- blue sea, green grass, dark trees, colourful flowers, shy animals
- great for both adults and children
- first and standard class (we and Celia's/Tim's dog bought a first class ticket)

Geography lesson: The British Isles

1. England, Great Britain, United Kingdom? One of the students has made a mistake. Find the mistake and correct it.

   Jonas "Next summer my parents and I are going to Manchester and Liverpool in England."

   Lisa "My English teacher says we should try to see other parts of Great Britain, too, not just Edinburgh and London."

   Yannick "My father has a friend in Dublin. Maybe I can visit him sometime. I have always wanted to go to the United Kingdom."

2. What is what in the British Isles?

   a) Watch the video and then colour the different countries: England (red), Scotland (blue), Wales (green), Ireland (orange), Northern Ireland (grey).

   b) Watch the video again and then circle the United Kingdom (black) and Great Britain (yellow).

3. Can you fool your classmates?

   Look at the example. Then write down three sentences with a mistake in one of them. Swap your sentences with your partner and then find the mistake in your partner's sentences.

   Giant's Causeway, near Belfast: The Giant's Causeway is near Belfast in Northern Ireland, so it's also in Great Britain. (false)

4. Each country has its own national flag. Which flag belongs to which country?

   a) Listen to the explanation. Colour the flags correctly and write down the name of the country or flag.

   b) Look at the flag of the United Kingdom in your textbook. Can you explain which flags are in it?

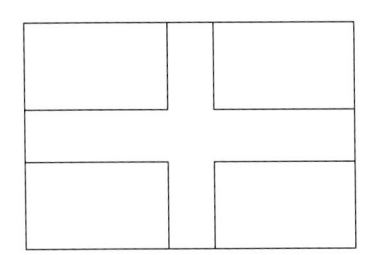

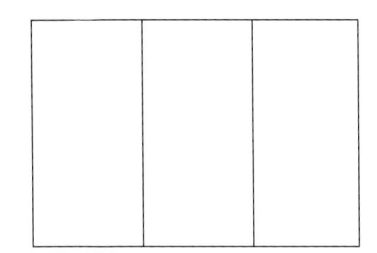

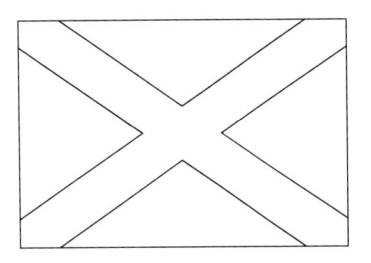

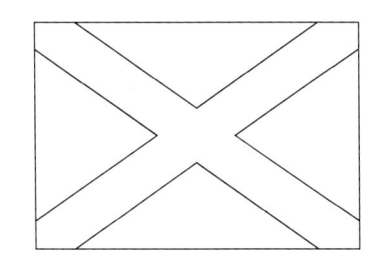

Shopping in London: Partner A

1. London is famous for its huge and exciting shops. But it also has some smaller and crazier shops.

   a) Set up your own shop. Here are a few ideas: a monsters' shop, a homework shop, a magic shop, etc. Then get together with a partner (B) and present your shop. The following phrases can be useful for your presentation:

   > The name of my shop is … • It is open from … to … • It is near … / on … Street •
   > My shop is special because … • You can buy … and also … • It/They cost(s) … • It is very important to … •
   > Thank you for your attention. Do you have any questions?

   b) Listen to your classmate's presentation and write down the answers to the following questions.

   Where in London is the shop?   When is it open?
   What can you buy at the shop? Why would/wouldn't you go to the shop?

2. Bargaining[1] at the flea market

   > You visit Camden Lock Market, a famous flea market in London. You want to buy a souvenir for your friend at home. There is this perfect but expensive sticker for your friend's schoolbag. It costs £2. Talk to the seller (Partner B) and try to get a better price. You have to buy this sticker!

   > Useful phrases:
   > "I'm interested in …"
   > "I like it, but…"
   > "Could I have it for £X?"
   > "Can you go any lower?"
   > "Is this the best price?"
   > "I'll need to think about it. I might come back."

   [1] **to bargain** feilschen, handeln

Shopping in London: Partner B

1. London is famous for its huge and exciting shops. But it also has some smaller and crazier shops.

   a) Set up your own shop. Here are a few ideas: a monsters' shop, a homework shop, a magic shop, etc. Then get together with a partner (A) and present your shop. The following phrases can be useful for your presentation:

   > The name of my shop is … • It is open from … to … • It is near … / on … Street •
   > My shop is special because … • You can buy … and also … • It/They cost(s) … • It is very important to … •
   > Thank you for your attention. Do you have any questions?

   b) Listen to your classmates' presentation and write down the answers to the following questions.

   Where in London is the shop?   When is it open?
   What can you buy at the shop? Why would/wouldn't you go to the shop?

2. Bargaining[1] at the flea market

   > You have a little stand at Camden Lock Market, a famous flea market in London. A German tourist (Partner A) wants to buy a sticker that costs £2 from you. Talk to the tourist and find a way to sell the sticker as expensive as possible. You have to sell this sticker!

   > Useful phrases:
   > "I'm interested in …"
   > "I like it, but…"
   > "Could I have it for £X?"
   > "Can you go any lower?"
   > "Is this the best price?"
   > "I'll need to think about it. I might come back."

   [1] **to bargain** feilschen, handeln

London Sights

1. From an old travel guide you have written down some things which you would like to do on your next trip to London. Is the information still up-to-date?
   Read the online information and cross out the wrong parts in your notes and write all the corrected notes in your exercise book.

> London Transport Museum: get in free; Covent Garden; history of London transportation (buses, trams, underground); open: 8 a.m. for 10 hours, closed: Sun
>
> Tower Bridge: check tourist information when bridge is up and down, nice sunset: 9 p.m. (July), get brilliant view
>
> London Dungeon: history museum of horror, near London Bridge Station, tours between one and two hours

---

London

London Transport Museum Learn about the history of London, its transport systems and the people who have travelled and worked on them. The collection features double-decker buses, trams and Tube trains. The queues to get in are usually shorter during the first hour of opening. There are many fun activities: You can even drive your own underground train on the simulator. The museum is interesting for boys and girls and a fun day out for the whole family.
Covent Garden Piazza; Mon-Thur, Sat, Sun 10 a.m. – 6 p.m.; Fri 11 a.m. – 6 p.m. Kids go free; Adults £17

Tower Bridge It's one of London's top landmarks[1]. The bridge opens and closes almost 1000 times a year. *Incredible!* The timetable can be checked online. The museum shows the history of the bridge and allows access to the bridge's top walkway. Don't worry, you don't have to take the stairs, there is a lift. You can also get a close look at the machine that raised the bridge for the first hundred years. On a sunny day, there is a great view of the city from the top, especially late afternoon or in the evening.
The museum and walkway are open from April to September between ten and six and from October to March between half past nine in the morning and half past five in the evening.

The London Dungeon Live actors, special effects and rides: Learn about the dark history of London without the boring bits. Meet one of London's infamous characters, Jack the Ripper, well known from movies and books. London Dungeon is a horror museum, a scary show and an interactive tourist attraction all in one. Take the 90-minute tour and pass through the Whitechapel Labyrinth, plague-ravaged[2] houses and the fearsome torture chamber[3]. Just a warning: The Dungeon is scary fun for everyone, except wimps! You can easily find the Dungeon near the London Eye (Waterloo Tube Station). See the website for opening hours. *Tip:* Go there around lunchtime when most tourists get a bite to eat somewhere else.
Recommended age: 12 years old and above.

1 **landmark** *Wahrzeichen* – 2 **plague-ravaged** *pestverseucht* – 2 **torture chamber** *Folterkammer*

---

2. Fill in the travel plan for a perfect day in London with your updated information and the texts.

	morning	noon/afternoon	evening
What?			
Why?			

Shakespeare's London

In the student newspaper at school you found an article about the city of London from Shakespeare's time.

London, wie es heute niemand kennt

Die Stadt London zu Shakespeares Zeiten war – verglichen mit heute – eine kleine Welt. Während des 16. Jahrhunderts wuchs die Bevölkerung
5 der Stadt auf ungefähr 200.000 Einwohner an. Zudem wurde sie auch für ausländische Besucher zusehends interessanter.

Londons Reichtum war eng mit der
10 Themse verknüpft, denn sie erfüllt ganz unterschiedliche Funktionen: Zum einen bot sie Anlegeplätze für Schiffe, die Waren in die Stadt brachten. Zum anderen stellte der Fluss
15 aber auch eine Nahrungsquelle zur Verfügung. Neben Fisch dienten auch Austern als Lebensmittel. Anders als heute galten Austern jedoch als Arme-Leute-Essen. Aus heutiger Perspektive würde man sicherlich zweimal überlegen, ob man etwas aus der Themse von 1600 essen möchte, denn sie stellte auch eine praktische Möglichkeit dar, das Abwasser zu entsorgen.

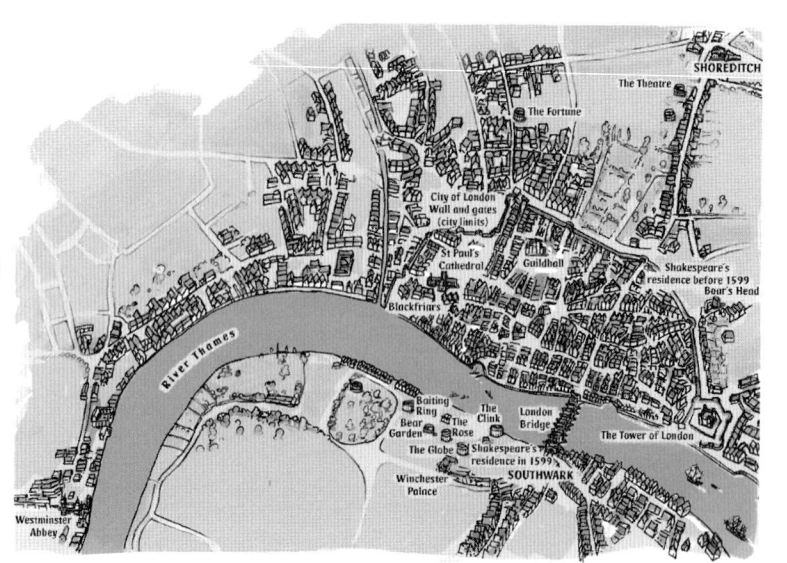

Die Stadt barg auch recht große Gefahren. Es gab weder Polizeistreifen noch Straßenlaternen. Besonders
20 ungemütlich konnte es außerhalb der Stadtmauern werden. Hier waren die wenigen Theater angesiedelt, die bei den Städtern sehr beliebt waren. Im Trubel um die Vorstellungen war es sehr einfach, das Publikum um ein paar Wertsachen zu erleichtern. Im Bezirk *Southwark* stand damals das berühmte *Globe Theater* von William Shakespeare. Die strengeren Gesetze der Stadt fanden hier keine Anwendung, sodass es allerhand Vergnügungsmöglichkeiten für das Stadtvolk gab. Die Theaterstücke waren wohl noch die
25 harmlosesten Möglichkeiten der Unterhaltung. Neben dunklen Tavernen gab es auch Bullen- und Bärenkämpfe.

1. Your penfriend Leo in Liverpool has to give a presentation on Shakespeare's London. Mark some interesting facts from the article which he could use to make his talk more interesting.

    Then write Leo an e-mail about what you have read in the article. Remember: Don't try to translate word for word. Just explain the key points.

2. Two boys got lost on a tour of Shakespeare's Globe. Watch the video. You don't have to understand every word they say. Write a diary entry of one of the boy's visit to the Globe Theatre.

    Useful words

    staging – *Inszenierung* • stage – *Bühne* • prop – *Requisite* • sword – *Schwert* • dungeon – *Verlies* • character – *Figur* • to haunt – *heimsuchen* • dull – *langweilig*

Whereabouts: London 24

Getting around and finding your way

1. Listen to the following London tourists who ask for directions. Will they get where they want to go? Follow the directions on the map to find out.

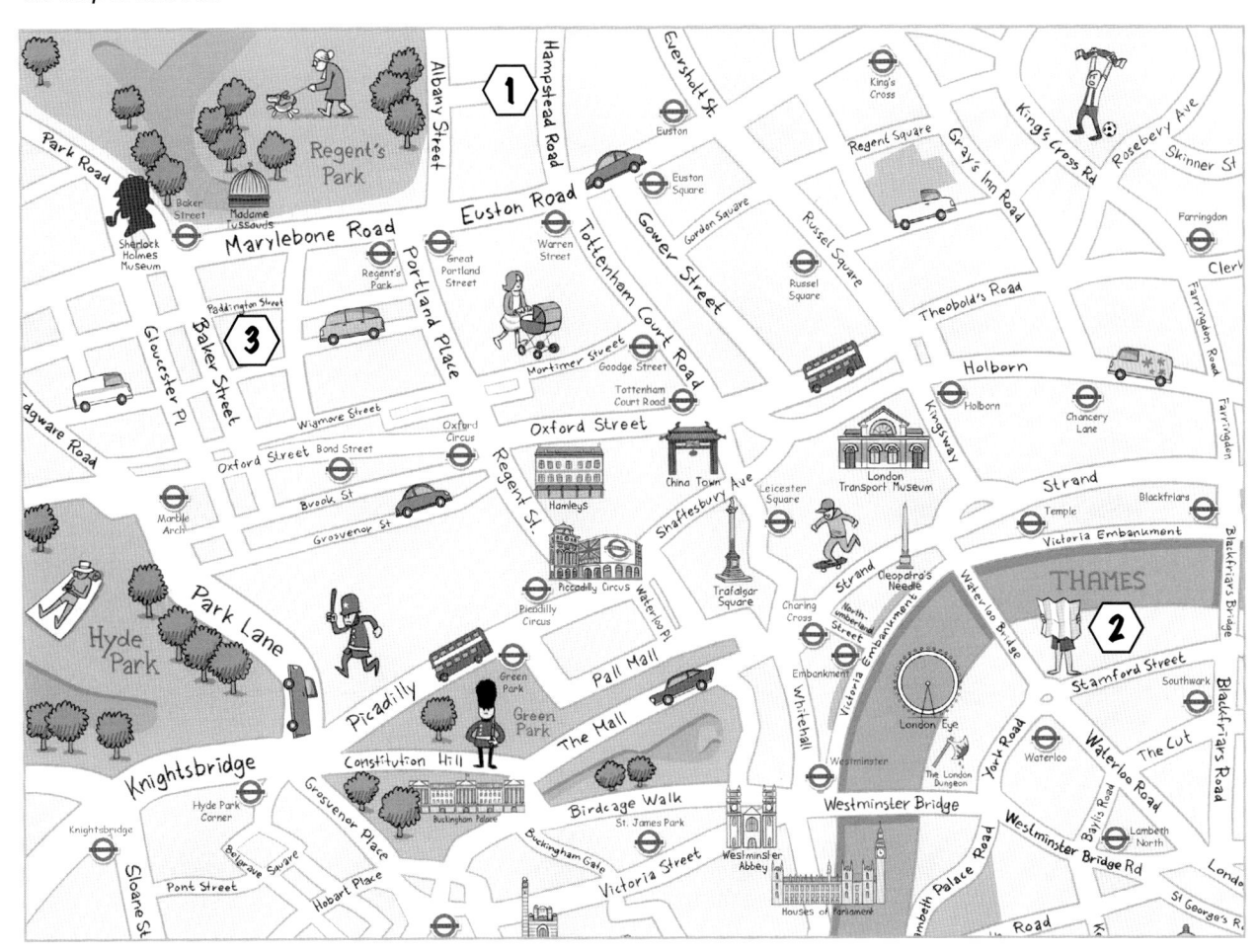

   Are the directions given in each conversation correct? Tick yes or no.

   a) The student wants to go to _____. Yes ☐ No ☐

   b) The woman wants to get to _____. Yes ☐ No ☐

   c) The man tries to get to _____. Yes ☐ No ☐

2. Watch the video about travelling in London and answer the following questions.

   a) With an Oyster Card you can use the Tube easily. True ☐ False ☐

   b) Everywhere in England you must stand in a queue but not in London. True ☐ False ☐

   c) In a pub, how do you know you can only get one more drink?

   d) What's in the video: How can you get around London?
      by bus ☐   by underground ☐   on foot ☐   by bike ☐   by taxi ☐   by car ☐

3. Practice the correct pronunciation of these words:

   Thames • Leicester • Greenwich • Burough

Edinburgh Castle – a guided tour

1. *Imagine you are on a holiday trip in Edinburgh with your family. Your younger sister doesn't speak English and your parents ask you to be her "personal language assistant". One afternoon you are taking a guided tour of Edinburgh Castle. Mediate what the guide says.*

   Guide Good morning, ladies and gentlemen! Welcome to Edinburgh Castle! I'm your guide for the next hour and I'm going to tell you many stories about the castle. Please stay close to me and follow me as we start our tour. Oh – and if you have any questions feel free to ask.

   You …

   Sister Kannst du ihn bitte fragen, ob man während der Tour Fotos machen darf?

   You …

   Guide Yes, of course. There are many great photo opportunities.

   You …

   Guide Edinburgh Castle was built nearly a thousand years ago. People have been inspired by it and many generations of Scottish monarchs[1] have lived here.

   You …

   Guide We have just walked through the castle gates and the small area here with the cannon is our first stop. This is called the One o'clock Gun. Every day, well except for Sundays, Christmas Day and Good Friday[2], a gun is fired at 1 p.m. – it's a very old tradition.

   You …

   Sister Oh, das ist ja eine interessante Tradition. Warum machen die das?

   You …

   Guide It was used to tell the time for people who did not have a watch. Today it's a tourist attraction. Let's move on to another highlight – the Great Hall. Once we are inside, have a look at the ceiling[3]. It is famous for its carved[4] stone heads and symbols. Also, there is a big collection of weapons[5] and armour[6]. The weapons were important to protect the Crown Jewels in the next building.

   You …

   Sister Kronjuwelen? Aber die sind doch im Tower in London!

   You …

   Guide No, these are different ones – they are the Scottish Crown Jewels. However, they are not part of this tour. But if you have the time, you should go and see them. You could also visit the National War Museum. There are many things to see at Edinburgh Castle.

   You …

   Sister Ach so. Alles klar. Das sind aber viele Möglichkeiten. Was sollen wir als Nächstes tun?

   1 **monarch** *Herrscher* – 2 **Good Friday** *Karfreitag* – 3 **ceiling** *Decke* – 4 **(to) carve sth** *etw schnitzen, meißeln* – 5 **weapon** *Waffe* – 6 **armour** *Rüstung*

2. *Act out the whole conversation together with two partners.*

3. *Find out more about Edinburgh Castle. Then write a similar dialogue to the one in task 1. Prepare to act it out in front of the class. Here are some sights you could also include:*

   Royal Palace • Prisons of War • The Stone of Destiny

Edinburgh Castle

1. Close your eyes and think of a castle. What does it look like? What can you hear? How does it smell? What can you feel with your hands? Describe what you can see, smell, hear and feel to a partner.

Edinburgh Castle

On a big rock above the capital of Scotland there is a huge castle – *Edinburgh Castle*. It is the most famous sight of the city and it attracts[1] visitors from all over the world. This monumental[2] building has inspired many people and royal families have lived there in former times.

5 It was also a military base with a secure jail[3] for prisoners of war. Today, the castle is home to different museums such as the *National War Museum* with a big collection of military artefacts[4] and paintings.

Most tourists who come to the castle want to see the *Scottish Crown Jewels*[5]. The queues can be very long and people sometimes have to wait for hours. When you finally enter the *Crown Room* you can see the *Scottish Crown Jewels*,
10 of course, but right next to them there is a big stone – *The Stone of Destiny*[6]. It is said that this stone played an important role in the coronation[7] of Scottish kings. There are many other legends about it too.

Visitors also come to see the *Royal Palace* with its fine rooms where kings and queens used to live. Mary Queen of Scots gave birth to her son James VI at Edinburgh Castle. He became King of Scotland in 1567 and King of England in 1603.

15 Near the entrance to the castle there is a small garden area with tiny gravestones[8]. If you look closely, you will notice that this is a cemetery[9] for dogs. Soldiers buried their pet dogs there and it is most likely one of the nicest animal cemeteries.

No tourist attraction would be complete without a gift shop[10] and a restaurant! Edinburgh Castle has six castle shops and two tea rooms. After experiencing Scottish history you can go there and enjoy a traditional afternoon tea.

1 **(to) attrackt sb** *jdn anziehen/anlocken* – 2 **monumental** *eindrucksvoll* – 3 **jail** *Gefängnis* – 4 **military artefacts** *Militärgegenstände* –
5 **Crown Jewels** *Kronjuwelen* – 6 **destiny** *Schicksal* – 7 **coronation** *Krönung* – 8 **gravestone** *Grabstein* – 9 **cemetery** *Friedhof*
10 **gift shop** *Geschenkartikelladen*

---

2. Read the text about Edinburgh Castle.

3. Tick true or false. Write down the line(s) where you found the information.

	true	false	line(s)
a) Edinburgh Castle is built on a big rock.	☐	☐	_____
b) People from different countries come to the castle.	☐	☐	_____
c) Tourists want to see the British Crown Jewels.	☐	☐	_____
d) King James was born in the castle.	☐	☐	_____
e) The small garden is a playground for children.	☐	☐	_____

4. Complete the sentences in your OWN words. Write the sentences into your exercise book.

   a) Edinburgh Castle is one of the most famous tourist attractions because …
   b) Tourists who want to see the Scottish Crown Jewels sometimes …
   c) When you have finished looking at the sights you can …

5. Which attraction of Edinburgh Castle do you find most interesting? Explain to a partner.

Whereabouts: Edinburgh

Scottish words

1. *"Kilt" and "wee" are Scottish words, which are used in English today.*
   Read the following Scottish words. Which of these words do you know?

nouns
Hogmanay [ˈhɒgməneɪ] traditional Scottish New Year's celebration
kilt [kɪlt] a skirt with many folds, made from tartan cloth and traditionally worn by Scottish men and boys
laddie [ˈlædi] boy
lassie [ˈlæsi] girl
loch [lɒk; lɒx] lake
porridge [ˈpɒrɪdʒ] food made from oatmeal *(Hafermehl)* boiled in water or milk, people eat it for breakfast
tartan [ˈtɑːtən] a pattern of different coloured straight lines crossing each other at 90 degree angles, or a cloth with this pattern
tattie [ˈtæti] potato
wain [weɪn] child

verbs
(to) haver [ˈheɪvə] (to) babble, talk nonsense
(to) keek [kiːk] (to) look
(to) ken [ken] (to) know

adjectives
auld [ɔːld] old
bonnie [ˈbɒni] pretty, beautiful
wee [wiː] small, tiny

2. *If you read a story about Scotland, you might find words in the text that are not common to other parts of the UK. These words make such stories more authentic and interesting. Write a story using 8 or more of the Scottish words from above.*

_____
_____
_____
_____
_____
_____
_____
_____
_____
_____
_____

3. *Read your story to a partner, then listen to your partner's story and count how many Scottish words they used.*

Whereabouts: Edinburgh 28

The Edinburgh Fringe Festival

1. Which festivals do you know? What kind of festivals are they – music, theatre? Are they in your region or somewhere else? Talk about these questions with a partner.

2. Let's find out more about the Edinburgh Fringe Festival.

> **Why is the festival called *Fringe*?**
>
> In 1947, eight theatre groups came to the *Edinburgh International Festival* but they were not part of the official programme. However, the artists[1] still performed in the city – not in the centre but on the fringe[2]. Every year more and more artists came to Edinburgh to perform in the festival and it has become one of today's most successful festivals.
>
> 1 **artist** *Künstler/in* – 2 **on the fringe** *am Rand*

Watch the video and decide whether the sentences are true or false. Correct the wrong sentences.

	true	false
a) The *Fringe Festival* is the largest arts festival on earth.	☐	☐
b) It takes place in September every year.	☐	☐
c) The festival is a good platform for international artists.	☐	☐
d) Artists can learn from seeing what other people are doing.	☐	☐
e) There are hundreds of shows.	☐	☐

_____

_____

_____

3. Watch the video again and complete the sentences in your OWN words.

   a) At the Fringe Festival you can see _____.

   b) The Fringe Festival is important because _____.

   _____

4. If you went to the Edinburgh Fringe Festival, what kind of show would you like to see? Explain your answer.

Welsh stars

1. Talk about the stars on this page. Who are they? What do you know about them?

Gareth Bale
- football star
- Real Madrid
- Wales national team

Christian Bale
- actor
- Hollywood
- *Batman Begins*

Ken Follett
- author
- from Cardiff
- historical novels

Duffy
- singer & songwriter
- from Bangor
- album *Mercy*

2. Prepare a presentation on one of the Welsh celebrities (or on another Welsh star you like). Follow these 5 steps:

Step 1: Look for information on the Internet and in magazines. Organise your information in a mind map or table. Here are some ideas about what you could try to find out:
- *Where and when was he / she born?*
- *Why is he / she famous?*
- *How did he / she become a celebrity?*
- *What are important facts about his / her life?*
- *What is special about him / her?*

Step 2: Put your information into a logical order.

Step 3: Create a poster with the information. The poster can have pictures, short texts and lists. You should also use a vocabulary box to help the class follow your presentation.

Step 4: Take notes for your presentation. Practise your speech. Use the *useful phrases* in the box.

Step 5: Hang up your poster in the classroom. Give your presentation.

Useful phrases:

to start the presentation: My presentation is about … / First, I'd like to say a few words about … / After that, … / And finally, …

to give the presentation: Here's a picture of … / This list tells you … / … means … in German …

to finish the presentation: Thank you for your attention. / Have you got any questions?

The Welsh flag

Wales is a country in the west of Great Britain and one of the four parts of the United Kingdom (along with England, Scotland and Northern Ireland). One of the most important Welsh symbols is the Welsh flag. It consists of a red dragon on a green and white
5 background.

The origin[1] of the dragon symbol on the Welsh flag is lost in history and myth[2]. It is possible that the Romans brought it to Wales around 50 BC. At that time Roman soldiers[3] carried a flag known as the 'draco', or dragon. After the Romans left
10 Britain, the dragon flag became a symbol of power for many rulers[4]. In the 5th century, for example, the Welsh king of Gwynedd had a 'draco' on his flag. But the dragon was not only an important symbol for the Welsh. In 1138 the Scottish adopted[5] it as a royal standard[6] and later King Richard I (also known as Richard the Lionheart) took a dragon flag on a crusade[7]. Some people also claim that the red dragon was the battle standard of the legendary King Arthur.

15 However, the dragon is often linked to the Welsh people in myths. A very popular myth tells the story of the brothers *Llud* and *Llefelys*. In early Welsh stories Llud is King of Britain and Llefelys King of France. When three plagues[8] beset[9] the British kingdom, Llud asks his wise brother for help.

One of the plagues is a terrifying howl[10], coming from a red dragon fighting a white dragon. In order to get rid of the dragons Llud digs[11] a pit[12] in the centre of the island and puts a pot of mead[13] in it. After a while the two dragons go into the pit, drink the mead and fall asleep. Llud then buries[14] the dragons in Snowdonia.

20 Many years later, Vortigern, a British king, wants to build a castle in Snowdonia, but every night the castle walls are destroyed. His magicians[15] tell him to kill a boy without a father and put his blood on the walls of the castle. Vortigern finds such a boy and wants to do what he has been told. But the boy asks him to dig a pit under the castle. As Vortigern does so the dragons are freed. They start to fight again and the red dragon wins. The child then explains that the red dragon stands for Vortigern's people, the white dragon for the Saxons. The red dragon became the
25 symbol of the Welsh people.

1 **origin** *Herkunft* – 2 **myth** *Sage, Mythos* – 3 **soldier** *Soldat* – 4 **ruler** *Herrscher* – 5 **to adopt** *übernehmen* – 6 **standard** *Standarte, kleinere Fahne* – 7 **crusade** *Kreuzzug* – 8 **plague** *Plage* – 9 **to beset** *heimsuchen* – 10 **terrifying howl** *schreckliches Heulen* – 11 **to dig** *graben* – 12 **pit** *Grube* – 13 **mead** *Honigwein/Met* – 14 **to bury so** *jmd. begraben* – 15 **magician** *Magier, Zauberer*

1. Read the text. Tick true or false. Write down the line(s) where you found the information.

		true	false	line(s)
a)	The Romans possibly brought the dragon symbol to Britain.	☐	☐	_____
b)	The Welsh flag has always been a symbol of the Welsh people.	☐	☐	_____
c)	According to the myth there are three plagues in France.	☐	☐	_____
d)	Llud uses a trick to get rid of the dragons.	☐	☐	_____
e)	The dragons get tired from fighting.	☐	☐	_____
f)	The dragons are buried for a long time.	☐	☐	_____
g)	Vortigern believes that if he kills the boy, the walls will not fall down.	☐	☐	_____
h)	The boy knows about the dragons under the castle.	☐	☐	_____
i)	The red dragon is a symbol of the Saxons.	☐	☐	_____

2. Write about the flag of your home country. What does it stand for? Since when has your flag been used?

Cardiff – Europe's youngest capital

1. Read the texts from brochures about sights in Cardiff, the capital of Wales. Explain to your partner which sight you would like to visit.

The Cardiff International White Water

Cardiff International White Water offers adventurers at all levels action packed activities including white water rafting, kayaking and river boarding. A *Family Rafting* session takes about two hours and it is the ideal activity for a fun day out with the family. Alternatively you can take it easy in the flat water area which offers a lot of fun paddle sports for everyone!
The CIWW is located in Cardiff Bay and easy to find.

Costs between £22.50 to £25 per person

The Grand Medieval Mêlée at Cardiff Castle

Have you ever seen a real knight? No? Then come to the medieval games at Cardiff Castle!
Watch fearless knights fighting the good fight until only one knight is standing at the Grand Medieval Mêlée! You can also learn about medieval life, about cooking and weapons. In addition, there are fun activities for families, like listening to stories from the Middle Ages and playing games from that time. Everyone gets to play a part in the day's action.

Adults £6; children £4

National Museum Cardiff

Visit the National Museum Cardiff and discover art, natural history and geology. The museum has a busy programme of exhibitions and events to amaze everyone.
In the Evolution of Wales gallery you can travel through time and find out more about the Big Bang and the formation of the earth. You will see moon rocks, meteorites, volcanoes and even dinosaurs!
Don't miss the Clore Discovery Centre where you can find hundreds of museum objects normally stored away. Have a close look at weapons, dinosaur bones and tropical insects. Use the microscopes and magnifiers to get the big picture and feel like a real scientist!

Admission is free!

2. You are on holiday in Cardiff. Write a postcard to a friend in Germany and tell him/her in German about …

   - the weather.
   - what you liked/disliked there.
   - the place(s) you have already been to.
   - what you will do next.

   Use the information from the brochures.

3. Think about a sight in your hometown or region.

   - Where is it and what can people do there?
   - Why is it a great place to visit?
   - What else is important to know about the sight (e.g. entrance fee, opening hours…)?

   Write a short text for an English tourist brochure. Find or draw a picture to put next to your text.

King Arthur and Rittha Gawr

1. What do you know about the legendary King Arthur? Collect your ideas in a mind map.

2. Listen to the story of King Arthur and the giant Rittha Gawr. Then tick the right answer(s). More than one answer can be correct.

   a) What is true about the giant?
   - [ ] Rhitta is said to have lived on top of Mount Snowdon.
   - [ ] He was very hairy.
   - [ ] He was a sad giant.

   b) What happened to the people of Snowdonia?
   - [ ] They were frightened of the giant.
   - [ ] They didn't care about the giant on the top of Mount Snowdon.
   - [ ] They fought against the giant but lost.

   c) What happened to the kings who didn't want to fight for Rhitta?
   - [ ] They were killed.
   - [ ] Rhitta took their beards and stitched them to his cloak.
   - [ ] They were driven out of the country.

   d) What kind of message did Rhitta send King Arthur?
   - [ ] "Give me your beard!"
   - [ ] "Fight against me!"
   - [ ] "If you don't fight for me, I'll kill you!"

   e) What did King Arthur do after receiving the message?
   - [ ] He ignored the giant.
   - [ ] He gathered his best men around him.
   - [ ] He rode for Mount Snowdon.

   f) What happened at the foot of Mount Snowdon?
   - [ ] Suddenly there was a snowstorm.
   - [ ] Sir Galahad was scared.
   - [ ] King Arthur wanted the knights to fight with him.

   g) How did the fight end?
   - [ ] The giant killed King Arthur.
   - [ ] Rhitta died in the snow.
   - [ ] The giant fell down the mountain.

   h) What did King Arthur do?
   - [ ] He rolled Rhitta down the mountain.
   - [ ] He ordered his men to bury the giant.
   - [ ] He said goodbye to his knights.

3. Imagine you are Sir Galahad. Write down the story from his point of view. Use the following ideas:

   - heard a lot about the angry giant
   - was scared
   - thunderstorm a bad sign
   - did not want King Arthur to go up the mountain
   - waiting was awful
   - hear nothing but the wind howling
   - suddenly the sun came out
   - King Arthur …

A trip to Chinatown

1. Look at the pictures from Chinatown in London. How are they different from other parts of London?

2. Chose one of the texts below and prepare a one-minute presentation. Get together with two partners and present your "Chinatown topic" to your group members. Then listen to the presentations of your partners.

3. Discuss: Which other pictures could go with the texts? What would you like to do if you could go to Chinatown? Is there anything like this in Germany?

The Chinese New Year

During the Chinese New Year you often hear *"Gung Hei Fat Choi!"* which means *"Happy New Year"*. The British start the New Year on 1 January and have New Year's Eve on 31 December. The traditional Chinese New Year, however, is based on a different calendar. It falls on the new moon between 21 January and 20 February. In 2016 the first day of the Chinese New Year was on 8 February. Chinese New Year is a 15-day celebration. People wear red clothes, in their houses they put up poems on red paper and children get money in red envelopes. Red stands for fire, which can drive away bad luck. Families come together for dinner and there are also beautiful fireworks. On the streets you can see dragons which sometimes stretch quite long. They are typically made of silk[1], paper and bamboo. Young men hold up the dragon on poles (long sticks) and dance through the streets.

1 **silk** *Seide*

An interview with a Chinese cook

In the following interview Eddie Lang, who teaches cooking at the School of Food, talks about his relationship with Chinese food.

Why is Chinese food important to you?
Eating together is very important in China. Here many people eat alone. But sharing food is much better than eating alone. I also like the way Chinese food is presented – it's important to decorate the whole table, not just present one plate of food nicely.

Who taught you to cook?
I watched my dad as he cooked. He often played a game with us. For example, if he made a soup, we had to guess what was in it. That way I learned how different things taste.

Is food an important part of a country's culture?
Absolutely. The British are very proud of their traditional dishes such as fish and chips. And the same is true for Chinese people. They have their own favourite traditional dishes.

What is your favourite food? Chinese or British?
This sounds really basic, but I'm a big fan of rice! The Chinese have so many different recipes for rice and there are many different types. I love them all.

Cultural difficulties

Life in the UK can be difficult for Chinese people who speak little or no English. Without the family nearby they can feel isolated and alone. This can be a real problem especially for the older generation, women who work at home and new arrivals. They are often unable to use public, social, health, welfare[2], educational and legal services[3]. Housing can also be a problem especially for people who work in restaurants. Often their job is connected to their flat or room. If they lose their job, they could end up homeless. Chinese community groups try to help people with these problems and bring the British and Chinese communities together. A good way to overcome cultural difficulties and promote integration is the Trafalgar Square celebration of Chinese New Year. It is an important date in London's Festival Calendar.

2 **welfare services** *Sozialleistungen* – 3 **legal services** *Rechtsleistungen*

Multicultural Britain

A story of success

Patak's Original

Lakshmishankar Pathak, called L.G. Pathak, was born in 1925 in India. His family was very poor. When his father died the family moved to Kenya in search of[1] a better life. And they found one after opening a shop selling Indian sweets to Indians who also lived in Kenya. By
5 1956, however, the political situation in Kenya was changing and L.G. and his young wife Shanta left for Britain. They arrived in London in a very cold winter in November 1956. Their journey had used up almost all of their money and the family had only five pounds left.

In London it was difficult for L.G. to find work. The only job he could get was cleaning sewers[2]. At this point Shanta
10 started making Indian sweets and snacks in the tiny family kitchen. Soon word spread[3] and many people came to buy her Indian food. L.G. and Shanta's young son Kirit made deliveries[4] all over London. He used the Tube because back then it was free for children under 11.

After a couple of years the Pathaks opened a small shop behind Euston Station in London. It sold all kinds of Indian food. After ordering too many vegetables one time, L.G. decided to pickle[5] some of the vegetables and sell
15 them in jars. The jars became a big hit right away because it meant you could get real Indian food in next to no time. Hence[6] the family started to sell other goods in jars, like spices and sauces.

The business grew and grew. Today there are about 700 people working for "Patak's" worldwide. In 2007 the family sold the company[7] to Associated British Foods for £200 million. The company supplies British curry houses with sauces, and sells ready meals to all supermarkets in the UK. You can also buy the sauces in German supermarkets

1 **in search of** auf der Suche nach – 2 **sewer** Abwasserkanal – 3 **to spread** (sich) verbreiten – 5 **delivery** Lieferung –
5 **to pickle** einkochen, einwecken – 6 **hence** folglich – 7 **company** Unternehmen

1. Read the text.

2. Tick true or false. Write down the line(s) where you found the information.

	true	false	line(s)
a) L.G. Pathak's family wasn't rich.	☐	☐	_____
b) In Kenya the family's life became better.	☐	☐	_____
c) L.G. met his wife Shanta in London.	☐	☐	_____
d) The journey from Kenya to England was expensive.	☐	☐	_____
e) Kirit started to work for the family's company when he was only a kid.	☐	☐	_____

3. Complete the sentences in your OWN words. Write the sentences into your exercise book.

   a) One day L.G. Pathak had a great idea. He …
   b) It became a story of success because …
   c) Today "Patak's" is a …

4. On the company's website L.G.'s granddaughter Anjali says: "Patak's isn't just a company to me and my family."
   Explain what she means by this.

Multicultural Britain

The Notting Hill Carnival

In your summer holidays you visited your exchange partner in London and he took you to the Notting Hill Carnival. It was a fantastic experience and in the evening you wrote some notes into your journal. These are your notes and pictures:

Der Notting Hill Karneval

- findet jedes Jahr am letzten Sonntag und Montag im August statt und dauert 2 Tage
- Geschichte: seit 1959; Protest gegen Gewalt gegen Einwanderer aus der Karibik; Karneval sollte zeigen, dass sie auch zu London gehören
- über 1 Million Teilnehmer ⇒ das größte Straßenfest in Europa!
- große Parade durch die Straßen von Notting Hill
- viele verrückte, bunte Kostüme mit Federn und Pailletten
- Steelband-Wettbewerb ⇒ sehr laut, aber super Stimmung
- leckeres Essen aus aller Welt, besonders aber aus der Karibik
- großartiges Erlebnis ⇒ ich will unbedingt noch mal hin! ☺

1. Your exchange partner has asked you to write a guest entry on his blog for his English followers. Write this blog entry and use your notes. Don't forget to write a headline.

31 Aug

posted by _____

1 Comment

2. Exchange your worksheet with a partner and read each other's blog entries. Give your partner a short feedback: **content** (amount of information; interesting information), **language** (correct use of language; style of language), **structure** (form of address; body; ending)

3. Which multicultural events do you know in your hometown, region or in Germany? Would you like to go to one of them? Talk to a partner.

Multicultural influences in Britain

1. Do you live in a multicultural city (a city with people from many different countries) or have you ever been to one? Where do your family and friends come from? Talk about these questions with a partner.

2. Let's find out more about multicultural influences in Britain. Here are some words you will need to understand the video:

> **population** people who live in a country
> **an ethnically diverse country** a country with people from many different countries
> **community** Gemeinde, Gemeinschaft
> **(to) originally come from overseas** ursprünglich aus dem Ausland kommen
> **wave** Welle
> **refugee** Flüchtling
> **migrant / immigrant** person who moves to another country
> **cultural variety** kulturelle Vielfalt
> **vibrant** lebendig

a) Watch the video and tick (✓) the correct answer.

Example:

Where do many people who live in Southall Broadway in West London come from?
☑ Asia   ☐ Scotland   ☐ Africa

1. The Notting Hill Carnival celebrates the …
☐ Spanish culture.   ☐ German culture.   ☐ Caribbean culture.

2. Sunny's father Avinda came to Britain from …
☐ Russia.   ☐ Kenya.   ☐ India.

3. In the project *"Open Cities"* school children from Cardiff in Wales took pictures of …
☐ animals.   ☐ food.   ☐ people and places.

b) Watch the video again and match the sentence halves.

1	Many British people's families		a	brought different cultures together.
2	The first big wave of immigrants arrived		b	most multicultural schools in Wales.
3	New community-based projects have		c	to become part of the community.
4	St Mary's school in Cardiff is one of the		d	by ship from Jamaica.
5	"Open Cities" is a project to help migrants		e	originally came from overseas.

3. In the video the reporter says: "The cultural variety makes Britain a vibrant place to be, but it's not without its problems." Explain what he means by this.

London Jeopardy

	London Places	London People	Getting around in London	London sights	London facts
200£	This part of the human body has 3.5 million visitors a year and gives you a great view of London.	This queen was born in London and is famous all over the world.	This is the side cars drive on in the UK and, of course, also in London.	It's long, it's only water and it runs right through London.	This city is actually Europe's third largest after Moscow and Istanbul.
400£	If the Queen invites you for tea, you will probably have to go there.	This actor was born in London and played a wizard in the Harry Potter movies.	Everyone can easily recognize the buses in London because they have this colour.	This French woman created a museum which is a very famous place for tourists to visit in London.	This person lives on Baker Street and works together with Dr Watson.
600£	This is London's most famous market area with stalls, shops, pubs and restaurants.	In July 2013 when this royal was born a newspaper said: "This is the world's most famous baby."	This is the London name for the underground train system.	Robbers and thieves must go there if they want to steal the Crown Jewels.	This is London's biggest airport.
800£	This place takes you on thrill-filled journey through London's bloody past with a mixture of live actors, special effects and rides.	This famous football star was born in London in 1975.	You will hear this expression often when you travel on the Tube. It means that you must watch out when you are getting on or off the train.	Tourists often think the tower or the clock has this name. But it is really the bell.	With 310 meters this is the tallest building in the European Union and you can find it near the river Thames.
1000£	It is the most famous and largest toy shop in London.	Say hello to this British hero at Trafalgar Square about 50 m above ground level.	This card makes travelling on the Tube and on the bus much easier.	In this famous church in London kings and queens are crowned.	This very well-known book by Charles Dickens is set in London.

A day in the life of a British girl

7:30 A.M.
My alarm clock goes off at 7:30. I get up and wake my brother Toby. He's four years younger than me and can be quite annoying sometimes. We live together with our mum.

8:00 A.M.
I have breakfast with my family. I usually have cereal with milk, fruit and orange juice. My favourite is porridge or eggs and bacon, which we usually only have at the weekends. I take a lunch bag to school and eat there.

8:45 A.M.
School starts at 8:45. I'm in Year 7. What I like most about school are art lessons and breaks. Today, during art class, I drew a picture with China ink. In the breaks, my friends and I chat, talk about other people at school or practice dancing. I really like dancing.

10:00 A.M.
In French we often talk about the city of Montpellier, France, where we have an exchange school. It is my first year of French, so I hope I will be able to talk properly with my exchange partner. I like French but my favourite subjects are English and Art.

12:00 P.M.
Lunch break! I really enjoy lunch with my friends. It gives us time to have a nice chat. I often have bacon and tomato sandwiches, crisps, an apple and a white chocolate chip bar for lunch. When it is not a school day, my mother sometimes takes us to a restaurant for lunch and afterwards we go shopping on Oxford Street.

3:30 P.M.
This is when school is out. I sometimes ride my bike to the park with my friends. On sunny days, we dance, listen to music and get ice cream.

6:00 P.M.
For dinner, if I'm lucky, we have my favourite meal, *Toad in the Hole*. That's a sausage baked inside Yorkshire Pudding batter. My mum, my brother and I sit around the table and talk about our day.

7:00 P.M.
After dinner – or tea, as we sometimes say – we practise music: piano for me, guitar for my brother.

8:00 P.M.
I like to relax before bedtime. I watch videos on YouTube, listen to music on my iPod Touch, read books, or play games on my mobile.

8:30 P.M.
Bedtime. I share a room with my brother. We have bunk beds. I sleep on the top bunk. When my brother annoys me too much I can throw a pillow or my teddy bear at him. This always works. I think next year we will move to a larger flat so we can each have our own room. I hope it won't be too far away.

A day in the life of a British girl

1. *Underline what's wrong, and then correct the sentence.*

   a) The girl's favourite meal is a cheeseburger with bacon.

   b) School is out at 3.15 p.m.

   c) In the art lesson she built a castle out of stone.

   d) She likes to play videogames on the Xbox.

   e) She wakes her mother in the morning.

2. *True or false?*

   a) She drinks apple juice for breakfast.

   b) She does her shopping on Cambridge Street.

   c) Her brother plays the guitar.

   d) She is in Year 7.

   e) Her brother's name is Robby.

3. *Answer the questions.*

   a) What's *Toad in the Hole*?

   b) Where is her exchange school (city!)?

   c) For how many years has she learnt French?

   d) What are her favourite subjects?

   e) Why does she enjoy lunch with her friends?

4. *Tick the correct answer or answers.*

   a) In the morning who or what wakes her up?
   - [ ] her alarm clock
   - [ ] her brother
   - [ ] her mobile phone
   - [ ] nobody

   b) What does she like to have for breakfast at the weekends?
   - [ ] eggs and bacon
   - [ ] fruit
   - [ ] cereals
   - [ ] porridge

   c) How does she get to the park?
   - [ ] by bike
   - [ ] by bus
   - [ ] her mother drives
   - [ ] on foot

   d) Tea is another word for what?
   - [ ] lunch
   - [ ] breakfast
   - [ ] a snack
   - [ ] dinner

   e) She sleeps …
   - [ ] in a large flat.
   - [ ] on the top bunk.
   - [ ] on the bottom bunk.
   - [ ] with a teddy bear.

Guess the word – Partner A

word	taboo words	Explain your word here. Don't use the taboo words.	Guess the word.
1) the Romans	(the Celts, win, lose)	1)	
2) the Celts	(the Romans, win, lose)	2)	
3) The London Eye	(wheel, London, fun)	3)	
4) the Tube	(underground, train, London)	4)	
5) Great Britain	(England, UK, country)	5)	
6) Christmas	(December, presents, tree)	6)	
7) London	(capital, city, England)	7)	
8) coast	(beach, sea)	8)	
9) double-decker	(bus, London, red)	9)	
10) festival	(party, fun, school)	10)	

Guess the word – Partner B

word	taboo words	Explain your word here. Don't use the taboo words.	Guess the word.
11) fireworks	(New Year's Eve, colourful, burn)	11)	
12) football	(sport, grass, eleven)	12)	
13) Guy Fawkes	(bonfire, Gunpowder Plot)	13)	
14) the Houses of Parliament	(London, sight)	14)	
15) island	(Isle of Wight, sea, water)	15)	
16) p.m.	(after, noon, a.m.)	16)	
17) Queen	(king, Elizabeth, woman)	17)	
18) Scotland	(north, UK, country)	18)	
19) capital	(city, big, London)	19)	
20) airport	(plane, fly, travel)	20)	

Snap it!

1. Place the cards face up on a table and stand around it. Make sure everybody can see the cards well.
   Listen closely to the song "This is my city". When you hear a word or phrase which is also printed on a card, you snap the card and keep it. Watch out! Not all the cards are in the song!

pavement	Shakespeare	see a show	go to a musical	double-decker buses
Hyde Park	Thames	Hamleys	Regent's Park	Tower Bridge
Marble Arch	Madame Tussauds	tea with the Queen	the Houses of Parliament	coffee with Prince William
the London Eye	Piccadilly Circus	Big Ben	shopping	Trafalgar Square
the Changing of the Guard	St. Paul's Cathedral	ride the Tube	Camden	Harrods

Kommentar mit Lösungen

1 💬 British Christmas traditions

Lernziele
- Lernstandsdiagnostik: vorhandenes Wissen aktivieren
- Interkulturelle Kompetenz: über unterschiedliche Weihnachtsbräuche sprechen

Material zweisprachiges Wörterbuch

Kommentar
Diese KV kann anstelle von KV 4 eingesetzt werden.

Aufgabe 1
Zur Einstimmung in das Thema tauschen sich die SuS über Weihnachtstraditionen aus. Dabei kann Vokabular vorentlastet werden oder alternativ schon hier der Umgang mit dem Wörterbuch geübt werden.
Boxing Day, candle, Christmas card / carol / Day / dinner / Eve / market / lights / tree, Father Christmas / Santa Claus, nativity scene, ornament, sleigh, tinsel …

Aufgabe 2
Die SuS lesen die Rollenprofile und schlagen unbekannte Wörter nach. Vier bis fünf SuS bilden eine Gruppe. Jeder übernimmt eine Rolle und gemeinsam spielen sie die vorgegebene Situation. Da die SuS ohne Skript miteinander sprechen, sollte der Fokus weniger auf Fehlerfreiheit sondern auf Kommunikation liegen. Eine Verschriftlichung des Dialogs ist als festigende Hausaufgabe denkbar.

Aufgabe 3
Im Anschluss an das Gespräch reflektieren die SuS über die verschiedenen Traditionen und tauschen sich über ihre Präferenzen und Interessen aus.

2 📖 Guy Fawkes

Lernziele
- Lesen: Sachtexte durch stilles Lesen erfassen und Informationen entnehmen
- Sprechen: eigene Verhaltensweisen u. Wünsche mit dem Partner austauschen

Aufgabe 1
Die SuS lesen sich die beiden Texte im Stillen durch. Die Lehrkraft leistet ggf. Hilfe bei der Vokabelerschließung.

Aufgabe 2
Hier wird die gezielte Informationsentnahme aus Texten trainiert. Gleichzeitig wird hier der Umgang mit Belegen geübt.

Lösung: a) true, text 1, line 3; b) false, text 1, lines 4–5; c) true, text 1, line 6; d) true, text 1, line 7; e) false, text 1, lines 11–12; f) true, text 2, line 1; g) true, text 2, lines 4–5

Aufgabe 3
Die SuS formulieren Quizfragen und beantworten sie gegenseitig. Hierfür kann auch das Video *The Story of Guy Fawkes* vorab gezeigt werden.

Extra: Im Internet gibt es einige (schülerfreundliche) Seiten mit weiteren Hintergrundinformationen zu Guy Fawkes. Die SuS könnten hierbei verschieden Aspekte des historischen Ereignisses recherchieren und, evtl. in Partnerarbeit, die Ergebnisse im Klassenverbund vorstellen.

Denkbar wären z. B. Plakate oder Präsentationen. Themenanregungen wären z. B. beteiligte Personen, King James, Houses of Parliament, Todesstrafe, Church of England / Catholics, eine Timeline …

Spooky Halloween

Lernziele
- Lernstandsdiagnostik: vorhandenes Wissen strukturieren und mit Informationen aus dem Sachtext verknüpfen
- Transferleistung: eigene Geschichte schreiben

Material Schulheft, Wörterbuch oder ausgedruckte Wortliste (Aufg. 3)

Aufgabe 1
Zur Einstimmung in das Thema schreiben die SuS ihr Vorwissen in eine Mindmap oder eine Liste. Schlüsselwörter: *sweets, trick or treat, USA, children, scary, dead people, pumpkin, etc.*

Aufgabe 2
Die SuS lesen sich den Sachtext durch und vergleichen und ergänzen ggf. Aspekte in ihrer Mindmap. Dies kann zunächst in Einzelarbeit erfolgen.
Im Anschluss können die Ergebnisse und der zweite Teil der Aufgabe in Partner- oder Gruppenarbeit verglichen werden. Ein gemeinsamer Austausch im Plenum ist ebenfalls denkbar.

Aufgabe 3
In Einzelarbeit schreiben die SuS eine gruselige Halloween-Geschichte. Dazu sollen so viele Adjektive wie möglich verwendet werden. In einer ersten Phase eignen sie sich die neuen Wörter an, z. B. mit Wörterbüchern. Alternativ kann die Lehrkraft eine Vokabelliste zur Verfügung stellen *(Download KV 3b/c)*, z. B. als Aushang an mehreren Stellen im Klassenzimmer. Die SuS können im Raum umherlaufen und sich die Adjektive notieren (→ Laufdiktat).

Eine Differenzierung nach Arbeitstempo und Niveau ist möglich, wenn man die Anzahl der zu verwendenden Adjektive festlegt. Eine andere Differenzierungsmöglichkeit wäre es, den lernstärkeren SuS eine unvollständige Vokabelliste auszuteilen und sie die Wörter im Wörterbuch nachschlagen zu lassen, während lernschwächere SuS mit der Lehrkraft die vollständige Vokabelliste durchgehen und dann bereits mit dem Schreiben der Geschichte beginnen.

Sobald die Geschichten fertig geschrieben sind, tauschen die SuS diese untereinander aus und bewerten ihre Geschichten gegenseitig auf einer vorgegebenen *Grusel-Skala*. Hier können auch mehrere Wechsel stattfinden.

Extra: Die SuS überarbeiten ihre Geschichten und erstellen ein Gruselgeschichtenband oder sie visualisieren ihre oder eine fremde Geschichte (fächerübergreifender Unterricht – Bildende Kunst).

Lösung: *KV 3b vollständige Vokabelliste als Download.*

Merry Christmas!

Lernziele
- Lernstandsdiagnostik: vorhandenes Wissen aktivieren
- Hör-/Sehverstehen: Fragen zu einem Filmbeitrag beantworten
- Interkulturelle Kompetenz: Informationen zu Weihnachtsbräuchen

Material Video *Christmas Scene 1* des British Councils

Kommentar

Diese KV kann anstelle von oder ergänzend zu KV 1 eingesetzt werden.

Aufgabe 1

Zur Einstimmung in das Thema sammeln die SuS in Einzelarbeit deutsche und britische Weihnachtstraditionen in einer Tabelle. Ein Austausch ist an dieser Stelle noch nicht notwendig. Die SuS ergänzen ihre Überlegungen in Aufgabe 3.

Aufgabe 2

Die SuS schauen sich den Film an und bearbeiten die Aufgaben. Je nach Leistungsstand der Lerngruppe kann der Film 2–3 Mal gezeigt werden.

Lösungen: *a): 1) true 2) false: There are Christmas markets in the UK. 3) false: People in the UK buy Christmas presents for their family. 4) true*
b): shopping; dinner; family; presents; Christmas; presents; food; hang up; Father; carrots

Aufgabe 3

Im Anschluss ergänzen die SuS die verschiedenen Traditionen in der Tabelle von Aufgabe 1 und tauschen sich über ihre Präferenzen und Interessen aus. Dies kann auch im Plenum geschehen. Eine schriftliche Hausaufgabe ist hier denkbar.

5 British food

Lernziele

- Sprechen: über typisch deutsche und britische Gerichte sprechen
- Präsentationstechnik: eine Kurzpräsentation gestalten und vorstellen

Kommentar

Diese KV zielt darauf ab, die Methodenkompetenz der SuS im Schwerpunkt „Präsentieren" zu schulen.

Anmerkung: Die SuS sollen als vorbereitende Hausaufgabe eigene Bilder von deutschem Essen machen oder im Internet suchen und ausdrucken.

> *Take pictures of a typical meal/typical meals you eat at home (breakfast, lunch and dinner) and bring them to class. You can take them yourself or find some on the Internet.*

Alternativ gibt es auch eine Zusammenstellung typischer deutscher Gerichte als *Download KV 5b*, die den SuS ausgeteilt oder als Folie präsentiert werden kann.

Aufgabe 1

Die SuS sprechen über ihre Lieblingsspeisen und erklären sie auf Englisch. Das benötigte Vokabular wird hierbei vorentlastet.

Aufgabe 2

Die SuS vergleichen ihre (ausgewählten) Bilder mit den Bildern der KV und notieren die Gemeinsamkeiten und Unterschiede. Sollten die SuS keine Bilder zur Verfügung haben, kann der Vergleich auch anhand ihrer Lieblingsspeisen erfolgen.

Bild 1 *lunch – sandwich (chicken, tomato, lettuce) and potato crisps*
Bild 2 *breakfast – "Full English Breakfast" baked beans, sausages, bacon, fried eggs, tomatoes, toast, butter, jam, cup of tea, orange juice*
Bild 3 *dinner – meat pie, green peas, carrots*
Bild 4 *dinner – "Fish and chips" fried battered fish, potato chips, mushy peas, tatar sauce*
Bild 5 *(afternoon) tea – "Cream tea" scones, jam, clotted cream, cup of tea*
Bild 6 *dinner – "Sunday Roast" roasted meat, roast potatoes, mashed potatoes, Yorkshire pudding, stuffing, vegetables (carrots, broccoli)*

Aufgabe 3
Die SuS bereiten eine Präsentation vor. Dabei beginnen sie bei den Unterschieden, die sie bei Aufgabe 2 bereits erarbeitet haben (Hilfestellung bes. für schwache SuS) und ergänzen neue Aspekte, wie in der Aufgabenstellung beschrieben (offenere Form bes. für starke SuS). Die Präsentationen können in kleinen Gruppen oder als *Gallery Walk* durchgeführt werden.

Tea Time
Lernziele
- Lesen: einen Sachtext über die Bedeutung von Tee in Großbritannien durch stilles Lesen erfassen und ihm Informationen entnehmen
- Sprechen: sich über eigene Verhaltensweisen und Wünsche austauschen

Aufgabe 1
Denkbar ist hier, dass die Lehrkraft den Text zunächst laut vorliest, dann unbekannte Wörter im Plenum geklärt werden und schließlich eine zweite Lektüre in Einzelarbeit stattfindet, die bereits die Aufgaben 2 und 3 in den Fokus nimmt.

Aufgaben 2 und 3
Diese beiden Aufgaben trainieren sowohl die gezielte Informationsentnahme aus Texten als auch das Paraphrasieren. Gleichzeitig wird hier der Umgang mit Belegen geübt.

Lösung für Aufgabe 2: a) true, line 1; b) false, line 3; c) true, line 5; d) false, line 11; e) false, line 13; f) false, line 18; g) true, line 19

Mögliche Lösungen für Aufgabe 3:
a) … the climate was much better there and it was cheaper.
b) … it is an old tradition to drink tea and there is a strong connection between the British people and tea.
c) … more coffee because there are many coffee shops.

Aufgabe 4
Diese Aufgabe ist eine offene Aufgabe, bei der sich die SuS über ihre eigenen Trinkgewohnheiten und Wünsche austauschen.

A British recipe – Shepherd's Pie
Lernziele
- Lesen: ein englisches Rezept verstehen
- Sprachmittlung: ein deutsches Rezept ins Englische übertragen

Material
Gegebenenfalls (verschiedene) Rezepte für Aufgabe 3, zweisprachiges Wörterbuch oder Online-Wörterbuch, z. B. *www.pons.eu*; *www.dictionary.cambridge.org*

Kommentar
Als Vorbereitung für die Aufgabe 3 sollten die SuS Rezepte auf Deutsch von (deutschen) Gerichten in den Unterricht mitbringen.

Aufgabe 1
Als Einstieg tauschen sich die SuS über ihre Koch- und Backgewohnheiten aus.

Aufgabe 2
Die SuS lesen die Zutatenliste und Zubereitungshinweise und notieren sich parallel unbekannte Wörter in ihr Heft. Dabei erleben sie, dass sich viele Wörter aus dem Kontext erschließen lassen.

Ergänzende Informationen zu *Shepherd's Pie*: Normalerweise ist es ein Gericht, um übriges Fleisch vom Sonntagsbraten (*Sunday roast*) zu verwerten. Wenn es mit Lammfleisch zubereitet wird, heißt es *Shepherd's Pie*, mit anderen Fleischsorten *Cottage Pi*e oder mit Fisch *Fisherman's Pie*.

Die SuS sollen die unbekannten Wörter nachschlagen. Dies sollte am besten in einem Online-Wörterbuch geschehen, da nicht alle „Schulwörterbücher" spezifisch genug sind.

Alternativ kann die Vokabeltabelle KV 7b *(Download KV 7b/c)* ausgeteilt oder auch großformatig im Klassenzimmer aufgehängt werden. Die vollständige Version *(KV 7b)* kann dabei entweder als Zeitersparnis oder als Differenzierungsmöglichkeit für lernschwache SuS eingesetzt werden. Wenn mehr Zeit zur Verfügung steht, eignet sich die unvollständige Vokabelliste *(KV 7c)* als Vorlage für Wörterbucharbeit.

Aufgabe 4

Nun die eigentliche Schreibaufgabe: Die SuS sollen ein deutsches Rezept ins Englische übertragen. Je nach Motivation der Klasse könnte dies der Beginn eines gemeinsamen englischen Kochbuches sein, das auch Übersichtstabellen von Maßeinheiten und Temperaturen beinhalten kann (dies wären mögliche Aufgaben zur Binnendifferenzierung).

British food culture

Lernziele
- Sprechen: über Erfahrungen in zusammenhängenden Sätzen sprechen
- Hör-/Sehverstehen: einem Video-Clip Informationen entnehmen
- Schreiben: Informationen aus verschiedenen Quellen zusammenfassen

Material Video *Food in Britain* des British Councils

Aufgabe 1

Zur Einstimmung (*pre-viewing*) sammeln die SuS ihr Vorwissen in einer Mindmap. Mögliche Aspekte: *fish and chips, crisps, muffins, tea, baked beans, bacon, toast, sandwiches, cold food for lunch, hot food for dinner, breakfast, beverage, …*

Aufgabe 2

Die SuS schauen sich den Film an und bearbeiten die Aufgaben. Je nach Leistungsstand der Lerngruppe kann der Film 2–3 Mal gezeigt werden.

Lösungen: *a) London's oldest food market, cheese, food writer; b) 1. Restaurants, world; 2. breakfast, everyone; 3. where, from; 4. different cultures*

Aufgabe 3

Im Anschluss ergänzen die SuS ihr Mindmap mit neuen Aspekten (z. B. *food from different cultures, Chinese brought oriental food …*). Darüber hinaus erklären sie, warum britische Gerichte neu erfunden werden. Mögliche Antworten: *British chefs are reinventing the dishes because they want people to still eat them. Maybe they are afraid that people will only eat new and trendy food like pizza or pasta because there are so many people from different cultures who bring their own food to Britain.*

Aufgabe 4

Bei dieser Aufgabe dürfen die SuS ihre Kreativität ausleben, indem sie ein Plakat erstellen. Eine Internetrecherche (Bilder etc.) bietet sich hier an. Die fertigen Plakate können in einem *Gallery Walk* präsentiert werden.

Extra: Die SuS werden angeregt, typisch britisches Essen in ihrer Umgebung zu suchen. Falls die Schulausstattung es zulässt, könnte die Klasse auch ein paar typische Gerichte in der Schule zubereiten (s. KV 7 Rezept).

Growing up royal

Lernziele
- Sprechen: einfaches Gespräch über die Familienbeziehungen führen
- Sprechen: über Vor-/Nachteile des Aufwachsens in einer Königsfamilie sprechen
- Sprechen: in altersgemäßer Form die eigene Meinung darlegen und begründen

Kommentar
Diese KV kann bereits früh im Englischunterricht der Unterstufe eingesetzt werden. Gerade Aufgabe 1 bietet sich für eine Wiederholung oder Vertiefung des Wortfelds „Familie" an, welches den SuS spätestens ab Klasse 5 bekannt ist. Der hier vereinfachte Stammbaum der britischen Königsfamilie kann alternativ auch der Ausgangspunkt für eine Internetrecherche zu den *Royals* sein. Möglich wäre hier zum Beispiel, dass die SuS die Biographien der Kinder von *Queen Elizabeth II* samt ihrer Familien recherchieren, als Steckbrief auf Plakaten sichern und anschließend präsentieren (z. B. in einem *Gallery Walk*).

Aufgaben 1 und 2
Als Einstieg in die Stunde sollen die SuS in Einzelarbeit versuchen, den Stammbaum der britischen Königsfamilie zu vervollständigen.

Lösung (von links nach rechts): *Queen Elizabeth II, Prince Philip, Princess Diana, Prince Charles, Princess Anne, Prince Edward, Prince Andrew, Camilla, Prince Harry, Prince William, Princess Catherine, Prince George, Princess Charlotte.*

Anschließend sollen sich die SuS in einem Partnergespräch über die vorgegebenen Verwandtschaftsbeziehungen Gedanken machen. Für schnelle Schülerpaare können weitere Konstellationen vorgegeben werden.

Lösung:
Partner A – *Prince George is Prince Charles' grandson. / Prince Philip is Prince Edward's father. / Princess Charlotte is the Queen's great-granddaughter.*
Partner B – *Camilla is Prince Harry's step-mother. / Prince William is Prince Andrew's nephew. / Princess Anne is Prince Philipp's daughter.*

Aufgabe 3
Aufbauend auf die Aufgaben 1 und 2 wird nun der älteste Sohn von William und Kate in den Blick genommen. Die SuS sollen sich in Gruppen über Vor- und Nachteile im Leben eines Prinzen austauschen. Das Ergebnis sollte in Stichworten gesichert werden. Mögliche Aspekte sind:

☺ advantages of growing up royal	☹ disadvantages of growing up royal
• having a lot of money/being rich • traveling to foreign countries • many fans • unlimited opportunities	• no privacy • always judged by the media/public • many duties • fake friends

Sollten die SuS für diese Aufgabe Hilfestellung benötigen, ist es möglich, die entsprechenden Symbole von *KV 9b* auf Folie zu ziehen und der Klasse als Ideenpool zu präsentieren. Das Arbeitsblatt kann alternativ auch nur an einzelne SuS / Gruppen ausgeteilt werden.

Aufgabe 4
Aufgabe 4 versetzt die SuS in die Rolle von George. Anhand der bereits erarbeiteten Vor- und Nachteile sollen die SuS nun ihre eigene Meinung äußern, ob sie gerne Mitglied der Königsfamilie wären. Diese Aufgabe kann auch als Hausaufgabe gegeben werden.

10 William Shakespeare – world-famous writer

Lernziele
- Sprechen: in zusammenhängenden Sätzen sprechen, Erfahrungen beschreiben
- Lesen: einen Text zu einem nicht bekannten Thema Lesen und erfassen
- Schreiben: zu einem Text in sprachlich korrekter Form auf Fragen antworten

Kommentar
Es bietet sich an, diese KV im Vorfeld zu einem der beiden KVs über *Shakespeare's Globe* in diesem Band zu bearbeiten.

Aufgabe 1
Zu Beginn (*pre-reading*) bietet sich ein Lehrer-Schüler-Gespräch an, in dem die SuS ermutigt werden, über ihre Lieblingsbücher und -autor/innen zu sprechen. Sicher werden hier auch englischsprachige Autor/innen, wie z.B. J.K. Rowling, genannt. Von hier aus kann dann zu William Shakespeare, dem bekanntesten Autor überhaupt, übergeleitet werden.

Aufgabe 2
Die SuS lesen den Text in Einzelarbeit still und beantworten die Fragen schriftlich. Dabei soll gleichzeitig das Anführen von Belegen (als Zeilenangabe) geübt werden.

▲ Bei lernschwächeren Klassen oder bei der ersten Beschäftigung mit diesem Aufgabentyp bietet es sich an, die Fragen und den Text für alle einmal vorzulesen. Anschließend sollen die SuS zunächst für jede Frage die Zeilen farbig markieren, in denen sich die Antworten auf die Fragen finden lassen. Hier kann die erste Frage an der Tafel gemeinsam gelöst werden, um allen zu verdeutlichen, wie die Aufgabe funktioniert.

Für SuS, die mehr Unterstützung benötigen, ist es denkbar, im Zimmer mehrere Kopien der KV aufzuhängen, auf denen jeweils die Zeilen mit den für die Antwort relevanten Informationen markiert sind. Auch können die SuS darauf hingewiesen werden, die in jedem Schulbuch befindliche Tabelle der *irregular verbs* aufzuschlagen, wenn sie Probleme mit der Bildung des *simple past* haben.

Lösung: a) *He was born in 1564. / He was probably born on 23 April 1564. (l. 3)*; b) *He learned Latin at grammar school. (l. 5)*; c) *Shakespeare was only 18 when he got married. (l. 6)*; d) *It is not known what he did for a living in his earlier years. Later he became an actor and playwright. (ll. 8–9, l. 12)*; e) *It was built near the river Thames. (l. 10)*; f) *Shakespeare's most popular tragedy is called Romeo and Juliet. (l. 14)*; g) *He was only 52 years old. (ll. 15–16)*

Aufgabe 3
Zuletzt sollen die SuS zu zweit über den Wahrheitsgehalt verschiedener Fakten zu Shakespeare spekulieren.

Lösung: *Richtig* a), b), d), e). Anmerkung zu a): Shakespeare hat in seinem Testament nicht angegeben, wer das beste Bett bekommen sollte. Es wird spekuliert, dass Shakespeare mit der Klausel des „second best bed" ausdrücken wollte, dass er in der Ehe unglücklich war. *Falsch* c) *About the time Shakespeare was born the first pencil was invented.* / f) *His mother called him „Will".*

11 Conversation with a Viking

Lernziele
- Sprechen: über eigene Vorstellungen zu einem Wikinger sprechen
- Schreiben: Fragen stellen/beantworten; über sich und die Familie schreiben
- Sprechen: einen bekannten Dialog phonetisch und intonatorisch richtig vorlesen

Kommentar

Diese KV kann bereits früh im Englischunterricht der Unterstufe eingesetzt werden. Sie kontrastiert das Leben der Wikinger in England um 1000 mit dem Leben der SuS und schafft so eine Brücke zwischen Geschichte und Gegenwart. Darüber hinaus wird das historische Wissen der SuS zur Geschichte Großbritanniens erweitert.

Aufgabe 1

Als Einstieg sollen die SuS zunächst in Einzelarbeit einen Wikinger zeichnen. Bei Zeitdruck reicht das Anfertigen von Skizzen aus. Es ist ratsam, den SuS einige Vokabeln anzugeben, die sie für das sich anschließende Partnergespräch benötigen, z. B. *(horned) helmet, axe, sword, beard, shield, hammer, fur coat*. Im nächsten Schritt sollen die SuS dann ihre Zeichnungen vergleichen (Partnerarbeit).
Hier kann die Lehrkraft das Partnergespräch unterstützen, indem verschiedene *useful phrases* an der Tafel vorgegeben werden, z. B. *My Viking wears… and his/her Viking has a…, This Viking has got a… That Viking hasn't got… but …, My Viking is (angry, happy, wild), whereas the other Viking is….*

Aufgabe 2

Nun lernen die SuS *Harold Harefoot* kennen. Die Hinführung zur Aufgabe kann durch eine gedankliche Zeitreise erfolgen, die folgendermaßen von der Lehrkraft formuliert werden könnte:

> *Let's go back in time. Imagine that we're all flying right now. We're leaving the classroom and are going up into the air. You're not afraid. It's fun and you're feeling free. We're crossing the English Channel now. Below us there are green hills. We're flying further north towards York. But York doesn't look like a modern city! You can see simple houses, stinky workshops and farm animals. Look! There's a Viking boy. He's waving at you. Maybe we should land and talk to him. He looks nice and friendly.*

Anschließend füllen die SuS den Dialog in Einzelarbeit aus. Es bietet sich an, unbekannte Vokabeln wie *adult, grown-up, raiders, wrestle, sagas, elves, trolls* vorzuentlasten.

> *Harold Harefoot* lebte von ca. 1015 bis zum 17.03.1040 und war der Sohn von *Cnut the Great*, der im 11. Jh. über ein nordisches Großreich herrschte, das England, Dänemark, Norwegen und Südschweden umfasste.

Aufgabe 3

Die SuS kommen mit einem Partner ihrer Wahl zusammen und üben die Dialoge. Dadurch vertiefen sie ihr Textverständnis und üben das dialogische Sprechen. Leistungsstärkere SuS können zudem zum freien Vortrag (ohne Ablesen vom Blatt) animiert werden. Wichtig ist hier, dass die Lehrkraft bei unbekannten Wörtern *(Aufgabe 2)* Hilfestellung im Hinblick auf die Aussprache gibt. Dies kann individuell oder im Plenum erfolgen.

Aufgabe 4

In Harolds Beiträgen finden sich mit *Hej, Far vel, elves* und *trolls* bereits vier Wörter, die den Einfluss der Wikinger auf die englische Sprache dokumentieren. In einer Internetrecherche können die SuS weitere Wörter finden, die aus dem Altnordischen ins Englische übernommen worden sind, wie z. B. *cake (from Old Norse „kaka"); husband (from Old Norse hūsbōndi wich means „householder"); knife (from Old Norse knīfr); Thursday (from Thor's day, the god of thunder); window (from vindauga, where wind means wind and auga is eye).*

Sherlock Holmes – Mrs Hudson's lucky day

Lernziele

- Hörverstehen: eine Erzählung verstehen und Fragen zum Inhalt beantworten
- Sprechen: in einfachen Sätzen Vermutungen zur Lösung eines Rätsels äußern
- Schreiben/grammatische Kompetenz: *conditional sentences type II*

Material Audio *Holmes*, Transkript KV 12b, *clues* KV 12c, Tisch KV 12d

Kommentar

Zum Einstieg kann das Vorwissen der SuS zu *Sherlock Holmes* aktiviert werden, indem z. B. im Unterrichtsgespräch bereits bekannte Fakten zum berühmten Detektiv in einer Mindmap an der Tafel gesammelt werden. Hier sollte kurz darauf eingegangen werden, dass die Geschichten im späten 19. und frühen 20. Jh. spielen, wenngleich es inzwischen neuere Adaptionen (z. B. von der BBC) gibt.

Aufgabe 1

Vor dem eigentlichen *Listening* sollten ggf. unbekannte Vokabeln vorentlastet werden, wie z. B. *famous, detective, case, to solve, landlady, first/second floor, to fight, to be missing, to be worried, weekly, to leave (a note), bridge (game), umbrella, clue, issue (of The Evening Standard)*. Auch sollten die SuS die Fragen bereits vor der Hörverstehensübung gelesen haben. Es bietet sich zudem an, den Text mehr als nur einmal vorzuspielen.

Aufgabe 2

Die SuS können diese Aufgabe in Partnerarbeit durchführen und zu zweit als Detektive rätseln, was mit *Mrs Hudson* passiert ist. Für die Lösung des Falls sind die Ausgabe von *The Evening Standard* sowie die drei Wettzettel von Bedeutung. Diese Gegenstände weisen darauf hin, was passiert ist:

> Mrs Hudson won all three games of bridge that day. Therefore she thought that it was her lucky day. She didn't go home but to a betting shop. There she bet on three horses. The first two times she wasn't lucky ("Duke of Sunshine", "Summer Sun"), but the third horse ("Gentle Rain") won the race. Suddenly she got 1000 pounds in her pocket! With the money she decided to go on holiday to Brighton. In no time she rushed back to her flat because the train to Brighton was leaving the same day. Since she was in a hurry she didn't have the time to write Sherlock a note. Instead she sent a postcard from Brighton. (Since the Royal Mail wasn't as fast as today the postcard hadn't arrived in London.)

Da das Rätsel nicht ganz einfach ist, kann als Hilfestellung *KV 12c* eingesetzt werden: Hier finden sich *clues* für die Lösung des Falls, die für alle kopiert und in Streifen geschnitten werden können. Die *clues* können dann z. B. verdeckt auf dem Lehrerpult ausgelegt werden, so dass sich die SuS, die nicht vorankommen, einen *clue* nach dem anderen holen können, um so Schritt für Schritt zur Lösung zu kommen. Optional kann die Lehrkraft eigene *clues* auf der KV ergänzen.

Aufgabe 3

Aufgabe 3 bietet sich als schriftliche (Haus-)Aufgabe an und stellt den Bezug zur Lebenswelt der SuS her. Sie kann als Wiederholung der *conditional sentences type II* eingesetzt werden.

13 A guided tour of the Tower of London

Lernziele

- Sprachmittlung: Sätze sinngemäß ins Deutsche und Englische übersetzen
- Sprechen: in einem Gespräch die eigene Meinung ausdrücken und begründen

Aufgabe 1

Das Bild der Londoner Skyline soll die SuS dazu animieren, zunächst die verschiedenen Sehenswürdigkeiten zu erkennen. Anschließend sollen sie sich in Partnerarbeit über ihre Vorlieben hinsichtlich der Sehenswürdigkeiten austauschen. Wichtig ist, dass die SuS ihre Wahl begründen.

Lösung (von links nach rechts): *Buckingham Palace, Westminster Abbey, the London Eye, the Houses of Parliament and Big Ben, Westminster Bridge, St. Paul's Cathedral, Trafalgar Square, the Gherkin, the Tower of London, Harrods, St. Margaret's Church*

Aufgabe 2
Es ist ratsam, dass die Lehrkraft die Aufgabe je nach Leistungsstand der Lerngruppe durch eine entsprechende Wortschatzarbeit vorentlastet und so die anschließende Sprachmittlung erleichtert. Anschließend sollen die SuS den Dialog drei Mal in verteilten Rollen lesen.

Bei leistungsstärkeren SuS ist es möglich, sie zu einem kleinen Schauspiel zu animieren, welches auch durch reale Gegenstände (Hut für den *guide* aus dem Theaterfundus der Schule o. ä.) angereichert werden könnte. SuS, denen das Auswendiglernen Spaß macht, können außerdem dazu aufgefordert werden, den Dialog frei vorzutragen.

Mögliche Lösung (Englisch):
- *Could we/Can we/Are we allowed to take (any) pictures?*
- *How many visitors come to see the Tower of London each year?*
- *How long do you have to wait/queue to see the Crown Jewels?*

Aufgabe 3
Diese Aufgabe knüpft an die Frage am Ende des Mediationstextes an. Hier können die SuS ganz individuell auf die Frage reagieren. Wichtig ist erneut die Begründung der Antwort.

Stonehenge of Scotland

Lernziele
- Leseverstehen: einen Sachtext zu einem noch nicht bekannten Thema erfassen
- Sprechen/Schreiben: zwei Touristenattraktionen miteinander vergleichen, dabei Steigerungsformen von Adjektiven verwenden

Kommentar
Zur Einstimmung kann den SuS das Bild auf der KV oder ein anderes Bild von den *Standing Stones of Callanish* gezeigt werden. Die SuS werden hier wahrscheinlich sagen, dass es sich bei den abgebildeten Steinkreisen um *Stonehenge* handelt, wodurch eine Überleitung zum Thema der Kopiervorlage geschaffen ist. Wahrscheinlich werden sie überrascht sein, dass es auch in Schottland (sogar viel ältere) Steinkreise gibt.

Aufgabe 1
Die SuS lesen den Sachtext in Einzelarbeit. Die anschließende Arbeitsphase kann in Partnerarbeit stattfinden. Eine Ergebnissicherung sollte dann im Plenum erfolgen (z. B. auf Folie). Eine originalgetreue Skizze findet sich auf der englischsprachigen Wikipedia-Seite zu den *Callanish Stones*. Von den SuS sollten vereinfachte Skizzen dieser Originalskizze erwartet werden.

Alternativ kann der Text auch von der Lehrkraft vorgelesen werden und anschließend gemeinsam die für die Aufgabe relevante Textpassage (Zeilen 15–21) markiert werden. Für lernschwächere SuS könnte die Lehrkraft (z. B. an einer nicht für alle sichtbaren Seite der Tafel) zudem ein Kreuz (ähnlich dem christlichen Kreuz) zeichnen. Diese Hilfestellung könnten sich die SuS anschauen, wenn sie nicht weiterkommen. Die SuS müssten dann nur noch den Text daraufhin lesen, wie viele Steine wo auf dem Kreuz liegen.

Aufgabe 2
Zur Vertiefung des Sachtextes sollen die SuS nun wichtige Fakten zu den *Standing Stones of Callanish* mit den in der Aufgabe gegebenen Fakten zum berühmteren *Stonehenge* vergleichen. Hierbei ist angedacht, dass die SuS die Steigerungsformen von Adjektiven sowie die in der Box angegebenen *useful phrases* verwenden.

Die SuS sollten zunächst die Fakten zu *Stonehenge* im Heft in einer Tabelle den Fakten zu den *Standing Stones of Callanish* gegenüberstellen. Anschließend können sie dann mündlich entsprechende Vergleiche anstellen, die zuerst in einem Partnergespräch, dann im Plenum geäußert werden. Es ist auch möglich, eine Verschriftlichung der Vergleiche zu fordern.

Lösung (Standing Stones of Callanish): *on the Isle of Lewis, built between 3000 and 2000 BC, 49 stones, largest stone 4,8 metres high, 40,000 visitors per year*

Aufgabe 3

Aufgabe 3 bietet sich als schriftliche (Haus-)Aufgabe an und stellt den Bezug zur Lebenswelt der SuS her.

15 Romans in Britain – life on Hadrian's Wall

Lernziele
- Sprechen: sich über den Inhalt eines Bildes auszutauschen
- Leseverstehen: einen Sachtext mit bekanntem Sprachmaterial verstehen
- Schreiben: einen Brief schreiben und über Gefühle und Ereignisse berichten

Material Landkarte von Großbritannien mit dem Verlauf des *Hadrian's Wall*

Aufgabe 1

Zur Einstimmung (*pre-reading*) bietet sich ein Lehrer-Schüler-Gespräch an, in dem die SuS ermutigt werden, über die im Bild dargestellten Personen, ihre Herkunft und ihr Tun zu spekulieren. Hier können die SuS ihr Vorwissen über die Römer anbringen, das sie bereits in der Schule oder privat erworben haben, z. B.: *Rome is now the capital of Italy, but more than 2,000 years ago it was the centre of the Roman Empire. The Roman Empire included most of Western Europe and the North African coastal region. The most famous Roman leader was Julius Caesar who was murdered in 44 BC. The Roman Empire was said to be one of the first democracies in the world, too.*

Aufgabe 2

Aufgabe 2 (*reading*) bietet den SuS wichtige Hintergrundinformationen zur römischen Invasion in Britannien allgemein und zum Hadrianswall im Speziellen, die sie für die Aufgabe 3 benötigen. Dabei sollten die Bezeichnungen „BC" und „AD" vorentlastet werden, um eine historische Verortung zu ermöglichen. Nach einer Phase des stillen Lesens können folgende Fragen zum Leseverstehen gestellt werden:

- *Which Roman general came to Britain twice? – Julius Cesar (55 and 54 BC) came to Britain twice.*
- *Why did Julius Caesar leave Britain? – The Celts fought him and won.*
- *Who invaded Britain in 43 AD? – Emperor Claudius' army invaded Britain.*
- *Who built a wall? How long is it? – Emperor Hadrian built it. It is 117 km long.*
- *What was life on Hadrian's Wall like? – It was a hard life because the soldiers were not used to the weather, for example.*

Aufgabe 3

Aufgabe 3 bietet einen produktionsorientierten Zugang zur Thematik. Hier sollen sich die SuS vor allem auf den letzten Absatz des Textes aus Aufgabe 2 beziehen und sich in die Situation eines römischen Soldaten versetzen, der am Hadrianswall stationiert ist (*post-reading, writing*). In einem Brief beschreiben sie aus der Ich-Perspektive, wie es ihnen als Legionär im fernen Britannien ergeht. Sie greifen dabei auf das in Aufgabe 2 bereits erarbeitete Wissen zurück und vertiefen es. Bei Bedarf kann diese Aufgabe durch eine Wiederholung der formalen Anforderungen an einen Brief vorentlastet werden.

Als Hilfestellung kann je nach Leistungsstand für ausgewählte oder alle SuS die *KV 15b* kopiert werden, auf dem der Brief als Lückentext zu finden ist. Er bietet den SuS Orientierung, schränkt sie aber auch in ihrer Kreativität ein.

Shakespeare's Globe

Lernziele
- Sprechen: Erfahrungen aus einem vertrauten Bereichen beschreiben
- Hör-/Sehverstehen: einem Video-Clip Informationen entnehmen
- Schreiben: Informationen zusammentragen u. in einem Text zusammenfassen

Material Video *Shakespeare's Globe in London* des British Councils

Kommentar
Es bietet sich an, diese KV im Zusammenhang mit der KV 10 zu *William Shakespeare* bearbeiten. Zeitbedarf: 60–90 Minuten.

Aufgabe 1
Zur Einstimmung (*pre-viewing I*) bietet sich ein Lehrer-Schüler-Gespräch an, in dem die SuS ermutigt werden, von ihren Erfahrungen mit Theaterbesuchen zu berichten. Vielleicht gibt es ja sogar SuS in der Klasse, die selbst Theater spielen. Hier sollten die entsprechenden Vokabeln eingeführt werden, z. B. *audience, auditorium, actor/actress, (main/centre) stage, costume, curtains, entrance, play, seat, trap door*.

Aufgabe 2
Aufgabe 2 bietet sich als Überleitung zum Video an (*pre-viewing II*). Hier wird gemeinsam in einem Lehrer-Schüler-Gespräch die Zeichnung des Globes betrachtet. Die Aufgabe soll den SuS eine erste räumliche Orientierung ermöglichen. Die SuS nutzen dabei die Beschriftung der Zeichnung, um das Globe mit ihnen bekannten Theatern zu vergleichen. Mögliche Aspekte können hier sein:

- There are no seats for the "groundlings" in the pit.
- The groundlings are very close to the stage in the Globe.
- There is no upper stage in most theatres today.
- Most of today's theatres have a roof and are not outdoor venues.

Nach dem Zusammentragen der wichtigsten Aspekte kann die Lehrkraft die SuS in einem Zwischenschritt dazu auffordern, ihre Eindrücke schriftlich zu formulieren, um die neuen Vokabeln zu festigen.

Aufgabe 3
Das Video ist Teil einer Serie von Clips, in denen die Figuren *Stephen* und *Ashlie* den Zuschauern Informationen über Shakespeare und das Globe vermitteln. Zum Video könnte wie folgt übergeleitet werden:

> *Let's find out more about the Globe. In the video there are Stephen and Ashlie. Stephen would like to be an actor and has got a job at the Globe. He and Ashlie go to the Globe to get Stephen's costume and to find out more about the famous theatre.*

Vor dem Anschauen des Videos sollten eine dem Leistungsstand der SuS entsprechende Vokabelvorentlastung stattfinden, z. B. von wichtigen Begriffen wie *acting/to act, (female) actor, character, costume, Hamlet, to perform, play, roof, stage, stage cannon*. Außerdem sollten die SuS die in der Aufgabe vorgegebenen Sätze kurz lesen und mögliche Verständnisprobleme im Vorfeld geklärt werden. In lernschwächeren Klassen kann das Video auch abschnittsweise geschaut werden (z. B. so, dass sich die SuS je nur auf zwei Sätze konzentrieren müssen).

Lösung: *a) true; b) true; c) false; d) true; e) false; f) false*

Aufgabe 4
Das Video wird noch einmal gezeigt. Dieses Mal sollen die SuS genau hinhören und die drei falschen Sätze aus Aufgabe 3 korrigieren.

Lösung: *c) The first Globe was built not far from the modern Globe. / e) The first Globe theatre burnt down during a play (Henry VIII). / f) Men and boys acted out the plays.*

Aufgabe 5

Die Aufgabe dient der Vertiefung des Wissens über Shakespeares Globe. Diese Aufgabe kann – je nach Zeitrahmen der Stunde – innerhalb des Unterrichts oder als Hausaufgabe gestellt werden. Alternativ wäre es auch möglich, die SuS Poster zum Globe erstellen zu lassen.

17 School uniforms – a necessary evil?

Lernziele
- Sprechen: Vor- und Nachteile von Schuluniformen sammeln und abwägen
- Sprechen: eine eigene Schuluniform gestalten und präsentieren
- Sprechen: sich über die schulische Kleiderordnung austauschen

Aufgabe 1

Die Bilder lassen sich gut als Folie (Download KV 17b) präsentieren. Als Hilfe können die SuS auf die *useful words* Bezug nehmen.

Muss unterschiedliches Vokabular noch eingeschliffen werden, kann in einem ersten Schritt „Find somebody who…" gespielt werden (z. B. „…is wearing black trousers."). Die SuS müssen in einem zweiten Schritt in ganzen Sätzen antworten: „He/She is wearing black trousers." Sollte dies Gegenstand des Unterrichts gewesen sein, lassen sich an dieser Stelle weitere Unterschiede zwischen britischen und deutschen Schulen ansprechen.

Aufgabe 2

Die SuS tauschen sich in Partnerarbeit aus und sammeln ihre Ergebnisse in einer Liste. Im Plenum werden dann weiter Argumente erarbeitet und gegebenenfalls diskutiert. Die SuS sollen ihre eigenen Listen dabei ergänzen.

pro: *no pressure to wear brands, attendance improves, less expensive (than designer labels), creates a sense of school/group spirit, less pressure in deciding what to wear, more discipline, easier to concentrate on lessons, less crime and violence in schools, more easily identify intruders*

con: *limits self-expression, leads to less desirable forms of self-expression (e.g. tattooing, piercing, etc.), diversity should be encouraged, initial / additional cost of uniforms, bullying in public / from different schools, enforcing rules is difficult / sanctions, boring and unfashionable, students don't like them*

Aufgabe 3

Die Aufgabe kann in Einzel-, Partner- oder Gruppenarbeit bearbeitet werden. Die SuS sollten angehalten werden, die Argumente von Aufgabe 2 zu berücksichtigen, da diese in die Präsentation einfließen können. Methodisch lassen sich die Ergebnisse in Form eines *gallery walk* auswerten. Auch könnten die SuS in einem Marktplatz ihre Entwürfe anpreisen (drei Durchgänge, jeweils ein Drittel der SuS öffnet einen Marktstand).

Aufgabe 4

Denkbar wäre eine Realisierung nach der Methode *Storm the board*: Die Lehrkraft notiert eine einfache Tabelle an der Tafel „Yes, I think school uniforms are a good idea." / „No, I don't think we should have school uniforms." Alle SuS stimmen mit einem Kreidestrich im entsprechenden Feld ab. Im Plenum wird diskutiert, was dafür bzw. gegen eine Schuluniform spricht. Die Gründe können ebenfalls als Tafelanschrieb gesammelt werden. Die Lehrkraft kann den SuS ein Gerüst zur Verfügung stellen („In my opinion …" / „The most important argument for me is…"). Die SuS sollen auf die Ergebnisse aus Aufgabe 2 zurückgreifen. Ausgewertet werden kann im *Blitzlicht*.

Aufgabe 5
Die Aufgabe sollte im Plenum bearbeitet werden. Leistungsstärkere Gruppen können versuchen, ein Regelwerk für Verstöße zu entwickeln. Mögliche Sanktionen, die diskutiert werden können: *extra work, detention, picking up rubbish in the hallways, parents come to school for a talk, suspension.*

Sean's day at school
Lernziele
- Leseverstehen: einen Brief zum Thema Schule erfassen
- Schreiben: einen Brief zum Thema Schule schreiben

Kommentar
Texterarbeitungsvorschlag: Die Methode des *traffic light reading* ermöglicht eine intensive Texterarbeitung. Die SuS unterstreichen Sätze, deren Inhalt sie verstehen in grüner Farbe. Gelb werden solche Sätze oder Wörter unterstrichen, bei denen die SuS Zweifel am Verständnis haben, Rückfragen haben oder sich unsicher sind. Im Wesentlichen verstehen sie aber die Aussage. Wenn Textteile auch nicht ansatzweise verstanden werden, sind diese rot zu unterstreichen. Diese Methode sollte etwa für das erste Textviertel gemeinsam geübt werden, um den SuS klarzumachen, dass nicht das Verständnis jedes einzelnen Lexems Voraussetzung für den Sinnzusammenhang ist.
Im Gesamten sollte gelten, dass die SuS die relevanten Stellen zur folgenden Aufgabenlösung im Brief markieren, bzw. am Rand kennzeichnen.

Lösung Aufgabe 1: a) 60 minutes, fun; b) you can put credit on them; you can get into rooms; c) three

Lösung Aufgabe 2: a) on the bus (Präposition!); b) six hours and ten minutes (Schultag = Unterricht + Pausen); c) chips, spaghetti, Shepherd's Pie (it's a meat pie with mashed potatoes)

Aufgabe 3
Die SuS schreiben einen Antwortbrief. Als Hilfestellung kann die Lehrkraft wichtige Aspekte zur Schule und zu einzelnen Fächern als Tafelaufschrieb festhalten. Nach dem Schreiben lesen ausgewählte SuS ihren Brief in Kleingruppen oder im Plenum vor.

Aufgabe 4
Mögliche Vergleichsaspekte, die dem Brief entnommen werden können, sind:

> *boys only school, number and age of pupils, way to school, (timetable) times, duration of lessons, ways attendance is checked, paying for food, spending time during breaks*

Als Differenzierungsmöglichkeit kann die Verschriftlichung in einem zusammenhängenden Text als Aufgabe gegeben werden.

A school trip to the Isle of Wight
Lernziel
- Schreiben: Eine E-Mail mit Urlaubseindrücken verfassen

Material *Map of Great Britain* (z. B. Karte im Textbuch)

Aufgabe 1
Als Einstieg kann die Karte von GB projiziert werden und die SuS finden die *Isle of Wight*. Stärkere Lerngruppen können dann, beginnend bei Portsmouth, über mögliche Schulausflugsziele beraten, beschreiben, wo sich diese befinden und die Gründe nennen, warum sie diese

gerne besuchen möchten. Die mündliche Durchdringung des Themas dient auch der Vorentlastung von Vokabular und Wendungen, die für die Schreibaufgabe hilfreich sind.

Lösung: *The Isle of Wight is/lies in the south of England. The nearest cities are Southampton and Portsmouth. There is a ferry from Southampton which takes you to the island. The Isle of Wight is located in the English Channel, only a few kilometres (about 6 km) off the coast of Hampshire, south of Southampton, east of Plymouth. It is the southernmost of the British Isles.*

Aufgabe 2
Grundsätzlich ist die Aufgabe je nach zu fördernder Schreibkompetenz leicht abänderbar (*blog entry, diary entry, letter, article for the student newspaper, …*), sofern die jeweiligen Textsortenmerkmale bekannt sind.

▲ Eine Differenzierung nach Leistungsstärke ist durch folgende Ergänzungen möglich:

Write about your two/three most interesting adventures. / What else did you see that is not in your notes? Add more funny or scary ideas. / Find out more about the Isle of Wight and write about another sight. What happened there?

20 Geography lesson: The British Isles

Lernziele
- die geografischen/politischen Bezeichnungen der *British Isles*; die Flaggen
- Hörverstehen: *listening for detail*

Material Video *The UK and Great Britain* des British Councils

Aufgabe 1
Als Hinführung zur Thematik bietet diese Aufgabe einen kommunikativen Zugang: Die SuS lesen laut die Aussagen vor. Der Fehler steckt in Yannicks Aussage, denn Dublin, die Hauptstadt Irlands, ist nicht Teil des Vereinigten Königreichs.

Aufgabe 2
Das Video bietet eine gute Gelegenheit die SuS auf unterschiedliche Seh-Stile vorzubereiten. Beide Schauspieler sprechen in natürlicher Geschwindigkeit, was eher ungewohnt und schwierig für die SuS sein dürfte, wenn sie jedes Wort verstehen möchten. Ziel der Aufgabe ist es jedoch, in zwei *watching for detail*-Aufgaben dem Video Einzelinformationen zu entnehmen.

▲ Möglichkeiten der inneren Differenzierung oder Weiterarbeit ergeben sich durch die Zusatzinformationen im Gespräch der Schauspieler. Ein Arbeitsauftrag für leistungsstarke SuS könnte lauten: „*What does the girl say about the Queen, the Prime Minister and the different parliaments?*" – *All the countries in the UK have the same Prime Minister and the same Head of State but Northern Ireland, Wales and Scotland have their own parliaments.*

Der Sprachumsatz kann erhöht werden, indem die SuS sich selbst in einer entsprechenden Präsentation versuchen, die als Hausaufgabe vorbereitet werden kann.

Aufgabe 3
Diese Aufgabe bietet eine gute Gelegenheit, die bisher im Lehrbuch kennengelernten Orte zu rekapitulieren. Die Lehrbücher bieten im Innenumschlag eine Karte der Britischen Inseln, auf denen häufig markante Orte verzeichnet sind. Im Sinne der integrierten Spracharbeit und je nach grammatischem Vorwissen der SuS kann die Lehrkraft auch abwechslungsreichere Formulierungen einfordern: *X lies in, X can be found in, X is located near, X can be visited in.*

Kommentar mit Lösungen

Aufgabe 4

Der Text sollte aufgrund der hohen Informationsdichte mindestens zwei Mal vorgespielt werden. Bei Bedarf kann das Vokabular vor Hören der Beschreibung vorentlastet werden *(Download KV 20b)*; mindestens das Wort *saltire* sollte den SuS ein Begriff sein. Je nach Leistungsstand der Klasse, kann auf die Flagge von Nordirland und *the Saint Patrick's Cross* gesondert eingegangen werden. Die walisische Flagge bietet die Möglichkeit das Vokabular zum Beschreiben von Bildern zu wiederholen.

Lösung: *a) Download KV 20b; b) The "Union Jack", the flag of the United Kingdom, is a combination of the flags of England, Scotland and the Saint Patrick's Cross.*

Shopping in London

Lernziele
- London als Stadt des Einkaufens kennenlernen
- Sprechen: Ideen für einen eigenen Laden entwerfen und präsentieren
- Rollenspiel: auf einem Markt um den Preis für Souvenirs feilschen

Kommentar
Als Einstieg in das Thema können die SuS auf London als „Einkaufsstadt" aufmerksam gemacht werden. Es gibt dort nichts, was es nicht gibt. Folgende Impulse können dabei genutzt werden:

- *Have you ever been to London? Did you go shopping? Tell your class where you went and what you bought.*
- *Do you know any famous department stores in London? What can you buy there?*
- *Do you know a famous market in London? What can you buy there?*

Mögliche Antworten: *Harrods (one of the most famous, biggest and most exclusive department stores in the world), Hamleys (one of the oldest, most famous toy stores in the world), Camden Market (one of London's largest markets as it is actually a number of several individual markets visited by half a million people a week)*
Die Aufgabe kann auch offener gestellt werden: „*What do you buy when you are on holidays?*" Als zusätzlicher Impuls kann über die britische Währung gesprochen werden, was die folgenden Aufgaben vorentlasten würde.

Aufgabe 1
Die Erarbeitung setzt an der Kreativität der SuS an und sollte explizit eingefordert werden (z. B. Vokabelhilfen, bzw. Hilfen zur Umschreibung).
Alternativ kann die Präsentation im Klassenverbund stattfinden und vorab in Partner- oder Kleingruppenarrangements eingeübt werden (z. B. *milling around, double circle*), bevor vor der Klasse gesprochen wird. Als zeitliche Richtschnur sollte eine Minute vorgegeben werden. Aufgabe b) als Vertiefung bietet die Möglichkeit, das Hörverstehen zu schulen. Eine tabellarische Lösung ist sinnvoll und lässt sich mit Aufgabe a) verbinden.

Aufgabe 2
Negotiating for a better price: Das Rollenspiel bietet diverse Differenzierungsmöglichkeiten (schriftliches Ausformulieren, Ausschmücken, Vorwegnahme des Gesprächsausgangs, offenes Ende, etc.) und Varianten der methodischen Ausgestaltung (*fishbowl*, stummes Schauspiel mit Synchronisation „von außen", frontale Präsentation, audio[visuelle] Aufnahme).

65

22 London Sights

Lernziele
- Leseverstehen: Informationen über Londoner Sehenswürdigkeiten überprüfen
- einen Ablaufplan für einen gelungenen Tag in London zusammenstellen

Kommentar

Als vorbereitende Hausaufgabe könnte den SuS aufgegeben werden, von zu Hause Reiseführer über London mitzubringen. Mit deren Hilfe könnte Aufgabe 2 ausgeweitet werden, indem die SuS weitere Tage in London planen.

Aufgabe 1

Als Einstiegsimpulse können diese Fragen gestellt werden:

- *When you visit a city what kind of sights do you want to see?*
- *What do your parents want to see?*
- *What do you think are typical parents' sights in London?*
- *How do you prepare for a trip? How can the Internet be useful?*
- *What's good about travel guides (books)?*

Lösung:

> London Transport Museum: ~~get in free~~ kids free, adults £17; Covent Garden; history of London transportation (buses, trams, underground); ~~open 8 a.m. for 10 hours, closed Sun~~ Mon-Thur, Sat, Sun 10 a.m.–6 p.m.; Fri 11 a.m.–6 p.m.
>
> Tower Bridge: ~~check tourist information when bridge is up and down~~ timetable online; ~~nice sunset 9 p.m. (July)~~ bridge is only open until 6 p.m. in July; get brilliant view
>
> London Dungeon: history museum of horror, take public transportation to ~~London Bridge Station~~ Waterloo Tube Station; tours between one and two hours long

Aufgabe 2

Die Tabelle erfordert ein tieferes Verhaken im Text und lässt sich auch gut in Partnerarbeit lösen, wobei zu beachten ist, dass nur teilweise die Abfolge vorgegeben ist und die SuS weitergehende sinnvolle Begründungen ableiten müssen (welche entsprechend differieren können).

	morning	*noon/afternoon*	*evening*
What?	London Transport Museum	London Dungeon	Tower Bridge Museum
Why?	shorter queues to get in	less crowded (other tourists eat lunch)	get a beautiful view of London at sunset

Als Fortführung ist eine Sprachmittlung denkbar:

„*Choose your most favourite sight from the worksheet. Tell your parents in German why you want to go there.*"

23 Shakespeare's London

Lernziele
- Sprachmittlung: einem Text Informationen entnehmen und ins Englische übertragen
- Hör-/Sehverstehen, Schreiben: basierend auf einem Videoclip einen Tagebuch-Eintrag verfassen

Kommentar
Als Vorarbeit kann KV 16 bearbeitet werden; andernfalls kann Frage 1 auf KV 16 als mündliche Einstiegsfrage dienen.

Aufgabe 1
Die Aufgabe bietet die Gelegenheit mit den SuS die Natur der Sprachmittlung im Gegensatz zur Übersetzung klarzumachen. Des Weiteren sollte ihnen bewusst werden, dass sie mit Umschreibungstechniken auch bereits komplexere Sachverhalte auf Englisch ausdrücken können.

Lösung: Beim Verfassen der E-Mail sollten die SuS darauf achten, die Quelle ihrer Informationen (*student newspaper*) anzugeben und auch weitere Aspekte der Adressatenorientierung zu berücksichtigen (z. B. „good luck with your presentation"; „do you have to give your presentation in English or history?"; „I don't really know much about Shakespeare, but I'd like to learn more"; ...)

Mögliche Fakten und deren Mittlung ins Englische mit dem Wortschatz von SuS im 6./7. Schuljahr:

- Shakespeare's London was a small world.
- There were about 200,000 people who lived in London. (Achtung: Schreibung der Zahl mit Komma!)
- The River Thames was very important: It was a place for ships to stop; the ships brought things for people who lived in the city; people could catch fish and oysters in the river.
- The River Thames was dirty.
- The city was quite dangerous. There were no police or street lamps. (auf Plural bei „police" in BrE hinweisen)
- Theatres were popular with people from the city.
- Thieves could easily steal money, for example, from the theatregoers.
- William Shakespeare's famous Globe Theatre was in Southwark.
- There were also bull and bear fights.

Aufgabe 2
Die Aufgabe ist anspruchsvoll, besonders für die Klasse 6. Daher sollte den SuS bewusst werden, dass sie für ein gutes Grundverständnis nicht jedes Wort verstehen müssen. Anhand der Bilder und dem Sprachmaterial können die SuS die Aufgabe mit ihren eignen sprachlichen Mitteln bearbeiten. Die SuS werden überrascht sein, wieviel sie tatsächlich schon verstehen können, wenn sie sich auf das Video einlassen.

Sollte eine entsprechende Infrastruktur vorhanden sein (z. B. ein Arbeiten im Computerraum), kann alternativ der Fokus dieser Aufgabe auf die im Video vorkommenden *short clips* von Shakespeares Werken gelegt werden. Diese sind auch als Animationen ohne Tonwidergabe zugänglich. Die SuS wählen ein Stück aus und erzählen die Geschichte mit ihren eigenen Worten (mit anschließender Präsentation). Diese erlaubt leistungs-, methoden- und zeitdifferenziertes Unterrichten und Individualisierung.

Getting around and finding your way

Lernziele
- Hören: Wegbeschreibungen verstehen und folgen (halboffene Aufgaben)
- Sehen/Hören: Fakten über London erfassen (geschlossene Aufgaben)
- Sprechen: Aussprache einiger geografischer Bezeichnungen beachten

Material 3 Audiodateien mit Wegbeschreibungen; Video *How to do London*

Aufgabe 1
Als Einstieg könnten die SuS wiederholend ihren Schulweg auf Englisch beschreiben und entsprechendes Wortmaterial kann an der Tafel festgehalten werden. In der *pre-listening* Phase

können die SuS auch Sehenswürdigkeiten auf der Karte identifizieren und von (1) bis (3) die Wege dorthin beschreiben.

24 b/c Aufgrund der komplexen Hörsituation sollten die Dialoge mindestens zweimal vorgespielt werden, wobei im ersten Durchgang lediglich die Zielorte aufgeschrieben werden und auf der Karte markiert werden sollten. Wird die Karte auf Folie kopiert *(Download KV 24c)*, können einzelne SuS die Grundlage für eine Besprechung darauf erarbeiten. Evtl. könnten in einer *post-listening* Phase Dialogteile besprochen und eingeübt werden, die eine freundliche Absage an die Touristen zum Inhalt haben, sofern man keine Wegbeschreibung zu geben vermag.

Lösungen: *a) the British Museum, yes; b) Hamleys, yes; c) Trafalgar Square, no*

Aufgabe 2
Das Video sollte in mehreren *viewing sessions* bearbeitet werden, wobei sich mehrere methodische Herangehensweisen empfehlen: *lend me your eyes, audio/visual only, dubbing*. Zudem stehen Untertitel in mehreren Sprachen zur Verfügung.

Lösung: *a) true; b) false; c) a bell is rung/a bell sounds; d) by bus (x) by underground (x) on foot (x) by bike (x) by taxi ( ) by car ( )*

Aufgabe 3
Die *post-listening* Übung fokussiert Wörter, die sich zum Sprachvergleich Deutsch/Englisch eignen, d. h. zur Veranschaulichung der (scheinbar) arbiträren Laut-Buchstaben-Zuordnung im Englischen und dazu, die Wichtigkeit der phonetischen Umschrift im Vokabelteil herauszustellen.

25 Edinburgh Castle – a guided tour

Lernziele
- Sprachmittlung: englische Sätze und Wendungen ins Deutsche übersetzen; einfache deutsche Fragen dem Sinn gemäß ins Englische übersetzen

Aufgabe 1
Die SuS schlüpfen in die Rolle von Besuchern des *Edinburgh Castle*. Im Rahmen einer Sprachmittlung ergänzen sie deutsche und englische Passagen.

Mögliche Lösung (Englisch):
- *Excuse me. My sister would like to know if she's allowed to take pictures.*
- *Could you tell us why the gun is fired every day?*
- *We thought the Crown Jewels were kept in the Tower of London.*

Aufgabe 2
Die Mediationstexte werden von jeweils drei SuS vor der Klasse oder in Kleingruppen vorgespielt. Es empfiehlt sich, den SuS genügend Vorbereitungszeit zu geben, um die Dialoge einzuüben. Sollte genügen Zeit vorhanden sein, kann der Dialog auch mehrmals mit wechselnder Rollenverteilung vorgetragen werden.

Aufgabe 3
Bei dieser Aufgabe sind die SuS gefordert, einen eigenen Mediationstext zu schreiben. Dabei sollen sie sich im Internet noch über weitere Sehenswürdigkeiten im *Edinburgh Castle* informieren. Dies kann in Einzel- oder Partnerarbeit geschehen. Sollten die technischen Voraussetzungen nicht gegeben sein, kann diese Aufgabe auch als Hausaufgabe bearbeitet werden.

▲ Leistungsstärkere SuS können auch eine Sehenswürdigkeit in ihrer Umgebung dafür verwenden. Die Ausgangssprache für diese Aufgabe wäre dann Deutsch. Folgende Aufgabenstellung wäre möglich:

Edinburgh Castle is a famous tourist attraction. What are popular tourist attractions near your hometown? Imagine you have an exchange student from England staying with you for a couple of weeks. You're taking them/him/her to see your chosen tourist attraction. Do some research and write a similar dialogue to the one in task 1. Prepare to act it out in front of the class.

Edinburgh Castle

Lernziele
- Lesen: einen Sachtext durch stilles Lesen erfassen u. Informationen entnehmen
- Sprechen: eigene Ideen und Wünsche mit einem Partner austauschen

Aufgabe 1
Diese Aufgabe soll die SuS gedanklich auf das Thema einstimmen. Denkbar wäre, dass dieses Gedankenspiel noch ohne KV von der Lehrkraft vorgestellt wird (kurze Fantasiereise). Wenn sich die SuS gegenseitig ihre Gedanken erzählen, werden eventuell Vokabelfragen auftauchen. Eine Option wäre, dass die SuS sich diese Wörter aufschreiben und die Lehrkraft im Anschluss im Plenum die Wörter bespricht.

Aufgabe 2
Die Lehrkraft könnte den Text zunächst einmal laut vorlesen, dann unbekannte Wörter im Plenum klären. Eine zweite Lektüre findet dann in Einzelarbeit statt, die bereits die Aufgaben 3 und 4 in den Fokus nimmt.

Aufgaben 3 und 4
Diese beiden Aufgaben trainieren sowohl die gezielte Informationsentnahme aus Texten als auch das Paraphrasieren. Gleichzeitig wird hier der Umgang mit Belegen geübt.

Lösung für Aufgabe 3: *a) true, line 1; b) true, line 3; c) false, line 8; d) true, line 13; e) false, lines 15–16*

Mögliche Lösungen für Aufgabe 4:
a) … you can see interesting things there such as the Scottish Crown Jewels, the Stone of Destiny, the Royal Palace and the National War Museum.
b) … have to wait a long time.
c) … go to a gift shop and buy presents or you can drink a cup of tea and get something to eat.

Aufgabe 5
Die SuS erzählen sich gegenseitig, welche Sehenswürdigkeit des *Edinburgh Castle* sie besonders interessant finden. Dabei können sie Informationen aus dem Text verwenden oder auf ihr Wissen von KV 25 zurückgreifen (sofern diese bereits eingesetzt wurde).

Scottish words

Lernziele
- Interkulturelle Kompetenz: den Zusammenhang zwischen schottischen und englischen Wörtern erkennen
- Schreiben: einen Text schreiben, der typische schottische Wörter beinhaltet

Material zweisprachiges Wörterbuch

Aufgabe 1
Die SuS lesen schottische Wortangaben und berichten im Anschluss, welche Wörter sie bereits kannten. Man könnte auch vorab an der Tafel in einer Mindmap schottische Begriffe sammeln – je nach Erfahrungsgrad der SuS.

Aufgabe 2

Die SuS schreiben eine eigene Geschichte und müssen dabei mindestens acht der vorgestellten schottischen Wörter verwenden. Zusätzlich sollten Wörterbücher zur Verfügung gestellt werden.

Evtl. müssen noch mehr Vokabeln vorgegeben werden oder die Lehrkraft sammelt im Plenum Ideen für eine Geschichte (z. B. *boy meets girl, seeing the Nessie, the Loch Ness monster*, …). Als Starthilfe kann ein erster Satz an der Tafel vorgegeben werden und die SuS schreiben alleine weiter.

Als Differenzierungsmöglichkeit könnte auch ein Lückentext ausgeteilt werden *(Download KV 27b)*, in dem lernschwächere Gruppen die fehlenden schottischen Wörter einsetzen oder englische Wörter durch schottische Wörter ersetzen.

Beispiel:

„*On a cold and rainy day, Ean, a young Scottish* laddie *from Aberdeen, woke up very early. He was still very tired but also hungry, so he got dressed and went downstairs to have his favourite breakfast:* porridge *with brown sugar on top. After breakfast he said good-bye to his mother and walked to the* loch *near his family's house because he wanted to meet his friend Ailsa. She was a* bonnie lassie *and Ean liked her very much. When he arrived at the* loch *he* keeked *around and there she was: she was standing next to an* auld *big tree and was wearing a red* tartan *dress. She saw him and smiled at him. …*"

Aufgabe 3

Die SuS kommen mit einem Partner ihrer Wahl zusammen und lesen sich ihre Geschichten gegenseitig vor. Die Aussprache der Wörter sollte gegebenenfalls nochmals im Plenum geklärt werden.

28 The Edinburgh Fringe Festival

Lernziele

- Lernstandsdiagnostik: vorhandenes Wissen aktivieren
- Hör-/Sehverstehen und Interkulturelle Kompetenz: Informationen aus einem kurzen Filmbeitrag entnehmen und Fragen beantworten

Material Video *Get ready for the Edinburgh Festival Fringe*

Aufgabe 1

Zur Einstimmung in das Thema tauschen sich die SuS über Festivals aus.

Aufgaben 2 und 3

Die SuS schauen den Film (02:58 Min) und bearbeiten die Aufgaben. Je nach Leistungsstand der Lerngruppe kann der Film 2–3 Mal gezeigt werden.

Lösungen Aufgabe 2: *true, false, true, true, false;* b) *It takes place in August every year.*; e) *There are thousands of shows.*

Lösungen Aufgabe 3:
a) … theatre, dance, music, cabaret shows.
b) … it is a place where people can connect with each other and it's fun.

Aufgabe 4

Im Anschluss unterhalten sich die SuS darüber, welche Art von Show sie gerne sehen würden, wenn sie das *Fringe Festival* besuchen könnten und geben Gründe dafür an.

▲ Differenzierungsoption: Wenn *Conditional Sentences (type 2)* bereits eingeführt sind, könnte diese Aufgabe auch als Wiederholungsübung eingesetzt werden. Die Lehrkraft schreibt einen

Beispielsatz an die Tafel und hebt die grammatikalischen Besonderheiten des *Conditional (type 2)* hervor. Die SuS sollten angehalten werden, mehrere Sätze zu erarbeiten.

If I went *to the Edinburgh Fringe Festival, I* would dance *to the music.*
if-clause **simple past**   main-clause **would + infinitive**

Welsh stars

Lernziele
- Sprechen: über Personen sprechen, die Identifikationsmöglichkeiten bieten
- Präsentationstechnik: gezielt Informationen aus dem Internet entnehmen
- Arbeitstechnik: die einfache Ordnungs- und Vernetzungstechnik der Mindmap zur Strukturierung von Informationen über einen Star verwenden
- Präsentationstechnik: eine Kurzpräsentation zu einem walisischen Star

Material Poster, dicke Filzstifte, Schere, Kleber, ev. buntes Papier, Wörterbuch

Kommentar
Die vorliegende Kopiervorlage zielt darauf ab, die Methodenkompetenz der SuS im Schwerpunkt „Präsentieren" zu schulen. Für die Internetrecherche (Aufgabe 2) sollten die technischen Voraussetzungen gegeben sein. Alternativ kann dieser Aufgabenteil auch als vorbereitende Hausaufgabe durchgeführt werden. Zeitbedarf: mind. 90 Minuten.

Aufgabe 1
Diese Aufgabe lenkt den Fokus der SuS auf die im Zentrum der Kopiervorlage stehenden walisischen Persönlichkeiten *Gareth Bale, Christian Bale, Ken Follett* und *Duffy*. In einem Lehrer-Schüler-Gespräch sollen die SuS zunächst sagen, was sie bereits über die vier Stars wissen. Hierbei können die Stichwörter aus den Steckbriefen bereits benutzt werden. Neue Vokabeln wie *actor (male and female actor)* oder *historical novels* können dabei vorentlastet werden.

Aufgabe 2
Aufgabe 2 hält die SuS zum eigenständigen Arbeiten an. Hier sollen die SuS allein oder maximal zu zweit zu einem der in Aufgabe 1 angeführten Stars eine Internetrecherche durchführen. Die angegebenen fünf Schritte sowie die *useful phrases* dienen dabei als Hilfestellung. Außerdem sollten bilinguale Wörterbücher bereitstehen, in denen die SuS unbekannte Wörter nachschlagen können. Möglich ist auch, dass leistungsstärkere SuS sich eine andere walisische Persönlichkeit aussuchen, die in Aufgabe 1 noch nicht vorgestellt wurde.
Am Ende des eigenständigen Arbeitens steht die Präsentation der Ergebnisse. Da dies im Plenum sehr zeitaufwendig sein kann, sollten die Präsentationen in einem *Gallery Walk* erfolgen. Bei dieser Präsentationsform hängen die SuS ihre Poster im Klassenzimmer auf. Einige SuS (z. B. jeder zweite) bleiben an ihren Postern stehen, während die anderen SuS im Uhrzeigersinn von Plakat zu Plakat laufen und sich einen Vortrag nach dem anderen anhören. Diese Methode hat neben dem geringeren Zeitaufwand den Vorteil, dass die SuS in einem kleinen Rahmen präsentieren, was die Aufregung mindert. Zudem tragen sie ihre Präsentationen mehrmals vor und erhöhen so den Sprachumsatz.

The Welsh flag

Lernziele
- Lesen: einen Text zur Bedeutung der walisischen Flagge erfassen
- Lesen: dem Text zur walisischen Flagge gezielt Informationen entnehmen
- Schreiben: einen kurzen Text über die Flagge des eigenen Herkunftslandes verfassen.

Material Schere, Tesafilm, Klebstift, zweisprachiges Wörterbuch

Kommentar

Als Einstieg in das Thema eignet sich folgende Aufgabenstellung:

Think about flags. What are they for? Why are they important? Talk about it in class.

Diese *pre-reading*-Aufgabe lenkt den Fokus der SuS auf die Bedeutung von Flaggen. Mögliche Antworten sind hier: *A flag is a symbol of a nation or a group (like pirates). It helps people to relate to a group.* Denkbar ist auch, dass die Aufgabe erweitert wird und die Lehrkraft fragt, welche Flaggen die SuS kennen (z. B. die Bundesflagge, den *Union Jack*, die *Stars and Stripes*…). Die Lehrkraft kann alternativ dazu verschiedene Flaggen als Realien oder als Bilder mitbringen und zeigen und so ein Quiz zu verschiedenen Flaggen (und den dazugehörigen Ländern) machen.

Extra: Anschließend kann – je nach Zeitrahmen – eine handlungsorientierte Aufgabe eingefügt werden, die sich mit dem Aufbau der walisischen Flagge beschäftigt. Dazu teilt die Lehrkraft den SuS die einzelnen Bausteine der Flagge als Arbeitsblatt aus *(Download KV 30b)* und fordert die Klasse auf, die Flagge richtig auszumalen und zusammenzusetzen. Dies macht den SuS erfahrungsgemäß viel Spaß, kostet aber Zeit (vor allem, wenn der Drache genau ausgeschnitten werden soll). Anschließend könnte man die fertigen Flaggen im Klassenzimmer aufhängen. Zeitbedarf: 60–90 Minuten.

Aufgabe 1

Aufgabe 1 hält die SuS dann zum genauen Lesen an. Gleichzeitig wird hier schon der Umgang mit Belegen geübt.

Lösungen: a) true (ll. 7–8), b) false (ll. 10–11), c) true (l. 16), d) true (ll. 18–19), e) false (l. 19), f) true (l. 20), g) true (ll. 21–22), h) true (ll. 22–25), i) false (ll. 24–25)

Aufgabe 2

Diese *post-reading* Aufgabe bietet sich – je nach Zeitrahmen – als Zusatzübung oder als Hausaufgabe an und kann mit einer Internetrecherche verknüpft werden. Hier sollten für die SuS Wörterbücher bereitgestellt werden, um ihnen das Nachschlagen unbekannter Wörter zu ermöglichen. Alternativ zur Recherche über die eigene Landesflagge ist auch die Recherche zu einer Flagge möglich, die in den landeskundlichen Kontext des Englischunterrichts passt. Beispiele sind der *Union Jack*, die englische, schottische und irische Flagge, das *Star-Spangled Banner*, die kanadische Flagge, die australische und neuseeländische Flagge.

Cardiff – Europe's youngest capital

Lernziele
- Sprechen: ein einfaches Gespräch über Sehenswürdigkeiten führen, dabei persönliche Meinungen ausdrücken und wichtige Informationen austauschen
- Sprachmittlung: geeignete Textausschnitte ins Deutsche übertragen
- Schreiben: vertraute Informationen über die eigene Stadt/Region in einer Tourismus-Broschüre zusammenfassen

Material zweisprachiges Wörterbuch

Kommentar

Vor der ersten Aufgabe wäre es möglich, sich dem Thema geographisch anzunähern. So ist es z. B. möglich, den SuS eine Karte des Vereinten Königreichs zu zeigen und sie die Hauptstädte von England, Schottland, Wales und Nordirland benennen zu lassen. Dabei sollte das Wort *capital* eingeführt werden, soweit es noch nicht bekannt ist.

Kommentar mit Lösungen

Aufgabe 1
Vor dem Lesen der drei Broschüren-Texte sollten von der Lehrkraft wichtige Vokabeln vorentlastet werden, z. B. *rapids, white water, raft, session, medieval, Mêlée, knight, weapons, to discover, evolution, formation, magnifier, scientist*. Anschließend erfolgt die Lektüre der Texte in Stillarbeit, bevor sich die SuS in Paaren über die darin vorgestellten Sehenswürdigkeiten austauschen.

Aufgabe 2
Aufgabe 2 nimmt die Sprachmittlung in den Fokus. Die SuS sollen sich vorstellen, dass sie ihren Urlaub in Cardiff verbringen und auf Deutsch eine entsprechende Postkarte an einen Freund/eine Freundin zu Hause schreiben. Dabei sollen sie schwerpunktmäßig bereits besuchte und noch zu besuchende Sehenswürdigkeiten vorstellen. Als Hilfestellung können den SuS Wörterbücher zur Verfügung gestellt werden, in denen sie unbekannte Wörter nachschlagen können.

Aufgabe 3
Diese Aufgabe dreht den Spieß um: Nun sollen die SuS mithilfe der angegebenen Fragen über eine Sehenswürdigkeit in ihrer Stadt/Region informieren. Falls die Fragen nicht *ad hoc* beantwortet werden können, können die Lücken in einer Internetrecherche während des Unterrichts oder als Hausaufgabe gefüllt werden.

In lernschwächeren Klassen kann die Lehrkraft die Aufgabe vorentlasten, indem für eine Sehenswürdigkeit in der Stadt/Region wichtige Stichworte mit den SuS in einem Gespräch gesammelt und an der Tafel (z. B. auf Moderationskärtchen) fixiert werden. Anschließend können die Stichworte gemeinsam in eine logische Reihenfolge gebracht werden. So entsteht ein Schreibplan, an dem sich die SuS beim Schreiben ihres eigenen Broschüre-Textes orientieren können.

Auch hier sollten Wörterbücher für die SuS als Hilfestellung zur Verfügung stehen.

King Arthur and Rhitta Gawr

Lernziele
- Sprechen: ein Gespräch führen, Informationen über König Arthus austauschen
- Hörverstehen: einem Hörtext über *Rhitta Gawr* Informationen entnehmen
- kreatives Schreiben: die Legende aus der Sicht von Sir Galahad wiedergeben

Material Audio *King Arthur and Rhitta Gawr*, Transkript KV 32b

Kommentar
Die Figur des König Artus ist in der walisischen Kultur und Sagenwelt fest verankert. Viele der Sagen über König Artus sind mit Orten in Wales verknüpft. So berichtet die vorliegende Sage von dem Kampf König Artus' mit dem Riesen Rhitta Gawr auf dem *Mount Snowdon*.

Aufgabe 1
Zur Einstimmung (*pre-listening*) bietet sich ein Lehrer-Schüler-Gespräch an, in dem die SuS ihr Vorwissen über König Artus äußern dürfen. Diese Aspekte werden in einer Mindmap an der Tafel gesammelt und von den SuS im Heft gesichert. Folgende Aspekte können hier zur Sprache kommen: *famous, many legends, not sure if he really existed, may have been a warrior-leader around 400 AD, Excalibur, Merlin, Knights of the Round Table (e.g. Sir Galahad, Sir Lancelot)* …
Um auf den folgenden Hörtext einzustimmen, ist es zudem möglich, als weitere *pre-listening activity* den Schauplatz der Sage, Mount Snowdon, auf einer Landkarte von Wales zu betrachten. Vielleicht lässt sich hier an bereits aus dem Unterricht vorhandenes Wissen anknüpfen.

Aufgabe 2
Bevor die eigentliche Aufgabe von den SuS bearbeitet wird, sollte eine Vokabelvorentlastung des Hörtextes erfolgen. Wichtige Vokabeln sind hier *cloak, beard, to bury so, giant, to fight,*

knight, loyalty, path, Snowdonia, to strike (struck), sword, thunderstorm, trophy, clap of thunder, to challenge.

Anschließend wird der Hörtext ein erstes Mal vorgespielt. Davor können den SuS bereits einfache Frage (*listening for gist*) gestellt werden, die im Anschluss an das erste Hören beantwortet werden sollen: *Who was Rhitta Gawr? What did he want from King Arthur? What did King Arthur do?*

Nach der Beantwortung der einfachen Fragen sollen die SuS dem Hörtext während eines zweiten Vorspiels gezielt weitere Informationen entnehmen und die Aufgabe 2 beantworten. Dafür könnte der Hörtext *(Download KV 32b)* auch noch mehrfach kopiert und im Zimmer aufgehängt werden, so dass gerade lernschwächere SuS nach dem Anhören noch eine weitere Möglichkeit erhalten, die Fragen zu beantworten. Alternativ kann der Hörtext auch für alle kopiert und bei der Ergebnissicherung zur Selbstkontrolle eingesetzt werden.

Lösung: *a) 1 + 2; b) 1; c) 1 + 2; d) 1; e) 2 +3; f) 1 + 2; g) 2; h) 1 + 2*

Aufgabe 3
Die letzte Aufgabe fordert die SuS zu einem einfachen Perspektivwechsel auf. Sie schlüpfen in die Rolle von Sir Galahad und erzählen die Sage aus seiner Perspektive. Je nach Leistungsstand der Lerngruppe können ergänzend zu den in der Aufgabe genannten Stichwörtern weitere Stichwörter in einem Lehrer-Schüler-Gespräch gesammelt werden, um die Aufgabe vorzuentlasten.

A trip to Chinatown

Lernziele
- Sprechen: Fotos besprechen, Unterschiede aus vorhandenem Wissen ableiten
- Präsentationstechnik: einem Text Informationen entnehmen und präsentieren

Aufgabe 1
Bevor die Vergleichsaufgabe bearbeitet wird, kann eine herkömmliche Bildbeschreibung Wortmaterial sichern. Als Vergleichsaspekte könnten Englischfestivals dienen oder typisch englisches Essen. Auf einer Karte, z. B. im Schülerbuch, kann Chinatown in London lokalisiert werden (*City of Westminster, Gerrard Street*, zwischen *Shaftesbury Avenue* und *Leicester Square*).

Aufgabe 2
Entweder nach Zufallsprinzip oder nach leistungsdifferenzierter Zuordnung (steigende Schwierigkeit der Texte) bereiten die SuS eine Kurzpräsentation vor und präsentieren diese in Dreiergruppen. Die Gruppen sind so besetzt, dass jeder Text einmal vertreten ist. Die Möglichkeit zum *peer-feedback* kann gegeben werden, indem eine aufgabengleiche Gruppenphase zur Übung vorgeschaltet wird. Die Lehrkraft kann an der Tafel eine engere Struktur für die Präsentation vorgeben (*introduction – answer wh-questions / give most interesting aspects – conclusion*).

Aufgabe 3
Die Leitfragen im Anschluss an die Gruppenpräsentationen können auch in ein Klassengespräch überleiten.

A story of success

Lernziele
- Sprechen: die persönliche Meinung zum Thema „Erfolg" ausdrücken
- Lesen: einen Sachtext über die Geschichte der Familie Pathak aus Indien durch stillen Lesen erfassen und ihm Informationen entnehmen
- Schreiben: das eigene Verständnis des Sachtextes erklären

Kommentar

Zum Einstig in das Thema kann den SuS folgende Aufgabe gestellt werden:

> *Think about success. How important is success to you? Where do you want to be successful (e.g. in school, in sports, …)? How can you become successful?*

Diese *pre-reading activity* führt vom allgemeinen und für die SuS mindestens aus der Schule bekannten Thema „Erfolg" zur Erfolgsgeschichte des Familienunternehmens *Patak's* hin. Die SuS sollen hier über die Bedeutung von Erfolg für das eigene Leben nachdenken und Wege zum Erfolg beschreiben. Die Aufgabe kann in einem Partnergespräch oder im Lehrer-Schüler-Gespräch durchgeführt werden. Je nach Leistungsstand der Lerngruppe kann es sinnvoll sein, an der Tafel Satzanfänge für die Antworten vorzugeben.

Mögliche Antworten:
- *Success is important to me because it makes me feel good.*
- *I want to be successful in school because then I can study whatever I want.*
- *If you are successful in your job, you will get rich.*
- *You can become successful by working hard.*

Aufgabe 1

Denkbar ist hier, dass die Lehrkraft den Text zunächst einmal laut vorliest, dann unbekannte Wörter im Plenum geklärt werden und schließlich eine zweite Lektüre in Einzelarbeit stattfindet, die bereits die Aufgaben 2 und 3 in den Fokus nimmt.

Aufgaben 2 und 3

Diese beiden Aufgaben trainieren sowohl die gezielte Informationsentnahme aus Texten als auch das Paraphrasieren. Gleichzeitig wird hier der Umgang mit Belegen geübt. Bei Aufgabe 2 kann a) im Plenum besprochen werden, um den SuS den eventuell neuen Aufgabentyp vorzustellen.

Lösung Aufgabe 2: *a) true, 2; b) true, 3–4; c) false, 6; d) true, 7–8; e) true, 11*

Mögliche Lösungen Aufgabe 3:
a) …*put vegetables in jars and sold them.*
b) …*for the first time people in Britain could buy Indian food and take it home / cook it at home.*
c) …*big business which sells Indian food all over the world.*

Aufgabe 4

Diese letzte Aufgabe ist eine offene Aufgabe und festigt das Textverständnis noch einmal. Erwartet wird hier eine kleine Zusammenfassung des Gelesenen auf einer abstrakteren Ebene, z. B.: *For Anjali Pathak the family's company is not only a place to work. It is also part of the family's history. She is proud of what her grandfather and father have achieved.*

The Notting Hill Carnival

Lernziele
- Sprachmittlung: deutsche Notizen in einen englischen Blogeintrag übertragen und dafür geeignete Informationen auswählen
- Feedback geben

Aufgabe 1

Die SuS werden in die Situation eingeführt und lesen „ihre" Notizen durch. Dann steht die Sprachmittlung im Vordergrund. Die SuS sollen sich vorstellen, dass sie gebeten wurden, einen Gasteintrag auf dem Blog ihres Austauschschülers zu verfassen. Die Notizen dienen als Grundlage. Evtl. sollte eine kurze Erklärung zum Aufbau eines Blogeintrags gegeben werden

(Download KV 35b) und auf die Kriterien für das *Peer-Feedback* (Inhalt, Sprache, Struktur) in Aufgabe 2 verwiesen werden.

Aufgabe 2

Nun sollen die SuS ihre Einträge mit einem Partner tauschen und sich gegenseitig ein Feedback geben. Dies kann schriftlich oder mündlich erfolgen, sollte aber den gängigen Feedbackregeln entsprechen. Für ein schriftliches Feedback kann auch eine Vorlage *(Download KV 35c)* verwendet werden. Das Feedback und die Überarbeitung des Blogeintrags (entweder des eigenen oder des Mitschülers) könnte als Hausaufgabe gestellt werden, je nachdem wie viel Zeit zur Verfügung steht.

Aufgabe 3

Den Abschluss bildet ein Gespräch über multikulturelle Ereignisse in Deutschland (Lebensweltbezug der SuS).

36 Multicultural influences in Britain

Lernziele

- Lernstandsdiagnostik: vorhandenes Wissen aktivieren
- Hör-/Sehverstehen und Interkulturelle Kompetenz: Informationen zu multikulturellen Einflüssen in GB einem kurzen Filmbeitrag entnehmen

Material Video *multicultural Britain* des British Councils

Aufgabe 1

Zur Einstimmung in das Thema tauschen sich die SuS mit einem Partner über ihre Erfahrungen aus. Je nach familiärer Situation und Wohnort können diese sehr unterschiedlich sein (evtl. ist an dieser Stelle ein Gespräch im Plenum sinnvoll).

Aufgabe 2

Vorentlastung neuer Vokabeln. Die SuS schauen sich den Film an und bearbeiten die Aufgaben. Je nach Leistungsstand der Lerngruppe kann der Film 2–3 Mal gezeigt werden.

Lösungen: *a) 1. Caribbean culture 2. Kenya 3. people and places / b) 1 e; 2 d; 3 a; 4 b; 5 c*

Aufgabe 3

Diese letzte Aufgabe ist eine offene Aufgabe und festigt das Textverständnis noch einmal. Erwartet wird hier eine kurze Gegenüberstellung von den schönen aber teilweise auch problematischen Aspekten einer multikulturellen Gesellschaft. Eine schriftliche Hausaufgabe ist hier denkbar. Je nach Reife der SuS kann eine geleitete Diskussion notwendig sein (s. Aufgabe 1).

37 London Jeopardy

Lernziele

- Fakten über London spielerisch festigen

Kommentar

Das *London Jeopardy* bietet sich am Ende einer Einheit über die britische Hauptstadt an. Da den meisten SuS das auf einer TV-Sendung basierende Quizformat nicht mehr bekannt sein dürfte, müssen ihnen mit einfachen Worten die Spielregeln erläutert werden:

> *Jeopardy is a quiz. Your job is not to answer the questions but to find the questions to the given answers. For example: "English." And your question would be: "What is your favourite subject?"*

The questions get harder the more money you can win. To select a category you say, for example, "London Places for 600 pounds, please."

Das *Jeopardy*-Spiel lässt sich über den Tageslichtprojektor spielen. Die Klasse sollte dabei in drei Teams aufgeteilt werden. Um den Sprachumsatz zu erhöhen, ist es auch denkbar, die Klasse zu dritteln, dann wieder je drei Teams zu bilden und jeweils Moderatoren zu benennen. Auch können einzelne Fragen mit Jokern (z. B. doppelte Punktzahl) vorab besetzt werden. Beim Spielablauf können die einzelnen Teams dann reihum eine Frage wählen und beantworten. Bei falscher Antwort wird der Betrag dem Team abgezogen und ein anderes Team hat die Möglichkeit zu antworten. Bei richtiger Antwort wird der Betrag dem Team gutgeschrieben. Alternativ kann auch mit einem *Buzzer* gespielt werden.

Grundsätzlich eignet sich die Erstellung eines Jeopardy-Spieles auch als komplexe Lernaufgabe (auch Partnerarbeit), um ein unterrichtetes Thema abschließend spielerisch zu festigen.

Lösungen:

London Places *What is the London Eye? What is Buckingham Palace? What is Camden Market? What is the London Dungeon? What is Hamleys?*

London People *Who is the Queen Elizabeth? Who is Daniel Radcliffe? Who is Prince George? Who is David Beckham? Who is Lord Nelson?*

Getting around in London *What is left? What is red? What is the Tube? What is "Mind the gap."? What is an Oyster Card?*

London sights *What is the Thames? Who is Madame Tussauds? What is the Tower of London? What is Big Ben? What is Westminster Abbey?*

London facts *What is London? Who is Sherlock Homes? What is Heathrow? What is the Shard? What is "Oliver Twist"?*

A day in the life of a British girl

Lernziele
- einen typischen Tagesablauf einer britischen Jugendlichen kennenlernen
- sich Informationen einprägen

Kommentar
Das vorliegende Lesespiel erfordert eine mikroskopische Lektüre der Textschnipsel von Seiten der SuS. Als Vorgehen empfiehlt es sich, die KV 38a zweimal auf DIN A3 zu kopieren und diese schließlich in einzelne Textabschnitte zu zerschneiden. Es entstehen so pro Seite zehn Schnipsel. Diese werden im Klassenzimmer gemischt aufgehängt bzw. ausgelegt. Die SuS werden in Zweierteams aufgeteilt, deren Aufgabe darin besteht, sich den Tagesablauf des britischen Mädchens möglichst genau durch Lesen der Schnipsel einzuprägen. Wichtig dabei ist es, zu wissen, dass die Lese-Aufgaben (KV 38b) erst nach der Lektüre der Textschnipsel ausgegeben werden. Die SuS dürfen sich keine Notizen machen, allerdings dürfen bzw. sollen sich die Schülerpaare untereinander absprechen, wie sie die Erinnerungsleistung am besten zu zweit bewerkstelligen (aufteilen, abfragen, Eselsbrücken, etc.). Lese- und Erinnerungszeit sollten zusammen nicht mehr als 15 Minuten betragen.

Die Auswertungsphase kann verschieden gestaltet werden, nachdem die Textschnipsel wieder eingesammelt sind. Entweder bekommen die Schülerpaare alle Fragen auf einmal ausgehändigt oder in Blöcken immer wieder das nächste Fragen-Set, sobald mindestens vier Fragen korrekt beantwortet sind. Um den Gewinner zu ermitteln, können die Antworten im Plenum besprochen werden und die SuS korrigieren ein gegnerisches Blatt. Jede richtige Antwort erhält *one credit*.

Lösungen:

1. a) <u>cheeseburger with bacon</u> *(correct: Toad in the Hole)*; b) <u>3.15 p.m.</u> *(3.30 p.m.)*; c) <u>built a castle</u> *(drew a picture with China ink)*; d) <u>the Xbox</u> *(her mobile)*; e) <u>her mother</u> *(her brother Toby)*

2. *a) false; b) false; c) true; d) true; e) false*

3. *a) It's a sausage baked inside Yorkshire Pudding batter.; b) Montpellier; c) It's her first year of French.; d) Her favourite subjects are English and art.; e) She enjoys lunch with her friends because she can chat with them.*

4. *a) her alarm clock; b) eggs and bacon, porridge; c) by bike; d) dinner; e) on the top bunk, with a teddy bear*

39 Guess the word

Lernziele
- Schreiben: Begriffe schriftlich präzise erklären

Material Schere

Kommentar
Das vorliegende Schreibspiel ist an das allseits bekannten Tabu-Spiel angelehnt.
Zwei SuS spielen zusammen, um sich gegenseitig schriftlich Begriffe zu erklären. Der Spielverlauf gliedert sich in drei Phasen:
In Phase 1 arbeiten beide SuS getrennt. S1 erhält die Begriffe 1–10, S2 erhält 11–20. Die SuS schreiben in die Erläuterungsspalte eine möglichst prägnante Erklärung ihres Begriffs, ohne die angegebenen *taboo words* zu verwenden. Hat ein Partner alle Wörter schriftlich erklärt, trennt er die linke von der rechten Tabellenhälfte an der gestrichelten Linie ab.

In Phase 2 tauschen beide SuS die rechten Hälften aus. Sie lesen die Erklärungen ihres Partners und versuchen das Lösungswort aufzuschreiben.

In Phase 3 wird aufgelöst. Jeder richtig erratene Begriff ergibt einen Punkt.

40 Snap it!

Lernziele
- Hören: einen Song über London hören und Details entnehmen

Material Video/Audio *Song about London*, *This Is My City*, *London Song*

Kommentar
Wie der Name schon sagt, geht es bei *Snap it!* darum, etwas zu erhaschen und zwar die ausgeschnittenen (und evtl. laminierten) Kärtchen.
Die SuS stehen in Gruppen (4–6 SuS pro Gruppe) um Tische, auf denen die Karten ausgelegt sind und dürfen eine Karte schnappen, sobald in dem abgespielten Song eines der Wörter/ Ausdrücke ertönt. Wer die meisten Karten geschnappt hat, gewinnt. Dazwischen müssen sich beide Hände hinter dem Rücken berühren.

▲ Spielvarianten/Differenzierung
Ohne die Wörter zu kennen, kann das Lied auch im vorab im Plenum abgespielt werden und besprochen werden, was Thema des Songs ist. Im Anschluss kann gemeinsam der Liedtext besprochen werden.

Die Lehrkraft stoppt alle 15–20 Sekunden und nur in der Pause dürfen Karten genommen werden. Falsch gezogene Karten ergeben Minuspunkte.

Lösung:

Snap it-Wörter mit Zeitangaben, wann diese im Song genannt werden: *pavement (0:04), Thames (0:06), Tea with the Queen (0:29), the Houses of Parliament (0:34), changing of the guards (0:37), ride the tube (0:45), Camden (0:58), double decker buses (0:59), Piccadilly Circus (1:01), see a show (1:21)*